Alissa Flierman

LIVING IN
YOUR TOP
1%

*Steve,
Thank you for being a top 1%
host. Wishing you many more
top 1% moments!*

Alissa

LIVING IN YOUR TOP

1%

Nine Essential Rituals to Achieve Your Ultimate Life Goals

ALISSA FINERMAN

For information about special sales and corporate purchases, please contact alissa@finermanliving.com

Cover design by Carlos Knight

Author photo by Nino Rakichevich

Interior book design by Carlos Moreno

Library of Congress Control Number 2010917517

ISBN 978-1-4536-1923-0

Printed in the United States of America

This book is dedicated to every person who has overcome or will soon overcome the word *impossible*.

CONTENTS

INTRODUCTION

There is no passion to be found playing small, in settling for a
life that is less than the one you are capable of living.

NELSON MANDELA

In 2001, I was living in New York City, frustrated by another cold winter, and working on Wall Street in a finance job that was not fulfilling. I wanted to be energized by my career and to feel like I was making a difference in people's lives. I wanted to be excited each morning and passionate about my work. Instead, I was emotionally drained. I felt stuck. I had invested so much time and effort in building my career but I was not where I wanted to be in my life. At the time, however, I did not see any other options.

There were two defining moments in my Wall Street career that eventually changed my path. The first was receiving my bonus at the end of my third year. I should have felt like I was on top of the world but instead I felt empty inside. The emptiness was a wake-up call that made me realize I was not connecting my passion with my work. My days as a corporate bond salesperson brought some of my most unfulfilling moments. Material things did not fulfill me; I wanted a career and a lifestyle I was passionate about. I took the Wall Street finance job because after earning my MBA, it seemed like something I *should* do. I did not know what my passion was, so I explored a high paying role in a world that intrigued me. I saw no downside in making this choice. From the outside, my life *looked* very successful.

The second defining moment of my finance career was getting laid off. It was one of the most crushing moments of my life, but ultimately a day that opened my mind to new experiences. I was working on the trading desk and received a call from my manager to come up to the human resources office on the eighth floor. Everyone's face went blank because they knew what was about to happen. No one said anything. My eyes connected with a co-worker on the trading floor and we both knew it was my last day at the firm. He did not say a word, but his eyes said, "I'm sorry." I was nervous when I stepped off the elevator, angry when I was laid off, and distraught when I left the office. I felt my world come apart. My reality was being redefined without my control, and it rocked my confidence. This was the first time I had ever been laid off and it was surreal. Everything happened in slow motion and I could not think clearly. The truth was: I was not enjoying the stress or early hours of my Wall Street job. As I look back, the layoff was a blessing in disguise.

I held two more jobs in the corporate world before I finally faced the reality that a career in finance was not the right path for me. One day, I received a postcard in the mail from New York University about an Executive and Life Coaching program. I never paid attention to advertisements, but something about this one in particular caught my eye. It had a catchy phrase about motivating others to follow their passion that caused me to read it more thoroughly. I was intrigued and wanted to learn more. I attended an information session and knew instantly that it was something I wanted to pursue. I left my position as a vice president of an investment company to enroll in the coaching program. Fourteen months later, I was a credentialed coach by the International Coach Federation and New York University. I finally felt energized and excited.

Leaving the finance world was a big leap and took a lot of courage. I was scared of giving up what I had worked so hard for and venturing into the unknown. The uncertainties were overwhelming at times. My journey truly began when I focused on what I love to do without thinking about all the obstacles. The turning point occurred when I listened to my inner truth and took one small step forward. Taking a chance turned out to be one of the best decisions of my life. It paved the way for me to move to California and finally explore my untapped potential as a writer, speaker, and motivational coach.

My life continues to be a work-in-progress. I stumble, like many of us, but I get back up. I make an effort to do one positive thing a day such as take a small step to grow my business, surround myself with winners, and enjoy life's little treasures.

My experience in changing direction midstream inspired me to write a book that encourages people to redefine their potential *regardless* of their current situation. I have met many people whose lives *appear* to be great on the surface. Upon getting to know them better, they often reveal that they are unfulfilled in their lives but too afraid to make a change. While some people are motivated to improve, others will settle for less than their best.

What is it that makes some people reach higher than others who are equipped with the same resources? The idea of living in your top 1% evolved from this question. The concepts shared in this book reflect knowledge learned from research, mentors, conferences, and experiences along the way. Some will be new ideas and others will be familiar to you. The value is in having these concepts translated into nine simple yet powerful rituals to help you create your personal roadmap to live in your top 1%. I will share success stories illustrating how the rituals make a difference and show you how to apply them to your own life. It is important to note there is a big difference between *knowing* about a concept and regularly *practicing* it. In order for you to make significant changes in your life, you will need to own these ideas and make them a part of your life.

This book is divided into three sections: *Assess, Create,* and *Implement.* Each section includes three rituals that will help you create the reality you want. The nine rituals will challenge you to think differently, take action, and get results. There is a *BOTTOM LINE SUMMARY* and an *IDEAS* page at the end of each ritual. I encourage you to take notes and jot down your reflections on the *IDEAS* pages as you read the book. There is also an *ACTION PLAN*, a *GOAL WORKSHEET*, and a *RITUAL WORKSHEET* included at the end of the book which will be useful in helping you make progress on your desired path.

It is my hope that this book will help you create a roadmap to explore your potential, inspire you to do what you love, and show you how to achieve moments of great fulfillment. I encourage you to keep an open mind, set your judgments aside, and think about what you *can* do. In examining your life, it is natural to feel frustrated, intimidated, and overwhelmed at times. Be patient and take one small step at a time. Get ready to change your life because this book is about making progress, no matter how big or small it may be. A great place to start is right where you are.

I believe you can shift your mindset to say "I can."

I believe you can choose "great" over "good."

I believe you can aspire to live in your top 1%.

Alissa Finerman

Santa Monica, California

December 2010

LIVING IN YOUR TOP 1%

If we did all the things we are capable of doing, we would literally astound ourselves.

THOMAS EDISON

How many people actually love what they do and enjoy their life *every* day? For some, parts of life are repetitious, parts are "have-to-do's," and parts are pure play. For most people, the pleasurable part is probably not as frequent as it could be.

From the time we are children, many of us are conditioned to win science fairs, sports games, or talent shows. We learn that we will be given medals, trophies, and other awards for a first place finish. We are trained to think that "winning" is based on being better than others. As we mature, we notice that the media showcases winners and often highlights the weaknesses of second and third place finishes. The Olympics celebrates athletes who are better than all the other athletes in the world. We learn that comparing ourselves to others extends globally. What about all the other contenders who did their best? After a while, it's natural to think that in order to be the best you have to be better than others. Many people define success by being in *the* top 1%, when in reality it's about living in *your* top 1%.

Looking back on your life, what are the moments that have brought you the greatest pleasure and a sense of *personal* achievement? Naturally, you will be proud of winning the Fifth Grade Spelling Bee or being chosen MVP of your high-school volleyball team. To begin expanding your mindset and thinking bigger, try to remember shining moments in your life that were *not* based on competition. Was it turning your photography hobby into a full-time career, raising money for a charity close to your heart, coaching your child's soccer team, or getting the promotion you worked day and night to achieve?

Often, we allow the beliefs we grew up with to dictate what we believe today. You may have mental maps in place that no longer serve you in different parts of your life. Some people are held back from reaching their full potential because of self-imposed limitations such as fear and lack of confidence. Others do not realize it is even an option to strive for something personally significant and exciting. People tend to have preconceived notions about what is possible and impossible. The best award is lasting personal fulfillment which comes from within. You can win gold every day by achieving your *personal* best.

You can live in your top 1% and enjoy moments of great success and satisfaction regardless of what other people around you are doing. Imagine what the world would look like if we all reached our greatest potential. Living in your top 1% is a win-win scenario. It's about living your best life and choosing the right road for *you*. It is not about attaining perfection or being better than others. Top 1% living is about having a vision, making progress in key areas, and understanding that small shifts in mindset produce powerful shifts in behavior. It is not dependent on your age, the size of your bank account, or your education. Top 1% moments are defined by the feelings of fulfillment, excitement, and joy that come from the *experience* of reaching for your best, rather than the accomplishments alone.

Living in your top 1% involves a *can-do* mindset, a passion to pursue your goals, and a resilience to bounce back when roadblocks surface. Every time you achieve something, no matter how small it may seem, you learn from the experience and gain confidence to face new challenges.

Living in your top 1% is seeing your world filled with potential and possibility. It may include your vision of becoming a professional athlete or running a profitable business, or it could include striving to be a great friend and parent, learning how to play the piano, or taking that art class. It's about what is most meaningful in *your* life. Regardless of where you are in your journey, you can apply these ideas. The quest starts by asking yourself, *"What does my top 1% look like?"*

LIVING IN YOUR TOP 1% DEFINED: The practice of using all your strengths, talents, and assets to live your best life possible. Living with this philosophy includes taking the words "can't," "should," and "impossible" out of your vocabulary and believing that you can create your reality. It is about reaching your personal best without comparing yourself to others. Top 1%ers see past roadblocks and take action.

Whether you are the CEO of a major corporation or an entry-level assistant, you can be living in your top 1%. Only you know if you are reaching your full potential. You must focus on ways to improve and make progress. The feeling of accomplishment comes from moving beyond your comfort zone and building confidence one step at a time.

Perhaps you think you are already where you should be and have nothing to improve. I respectfully challenge you to ask yourself if you are merely in a comfortable routine where you know what to expect, or if you are living a life that you love?

What does a great life look like to you? When you wake up in the morning are you excited about your day? Do the projects you are working on inspire you? What do you hear each morning? Do you hear the sound of the ocean waves, the birds chirping, children playing, or cars honking? What do you see? Do you look out to the trees, the street, or the city skyline? Do your surroundings work for you or do you dream of something different?

What values are connected with your ideal life? If being a great parent is important to you, do you make time to read to your children each night or spend quality time with them? If being healthy matters to you, are you making time to exercise and eat well? There are no *right* or *wrong* answers, only the ones that resonate with you.

For some, the idea of living in your top 1% may seem like an overwhelming or unattainable quest. Remember, everyone's top 1% moments will be different. Perhaps paying your rent or holding a steady job is a top 1% moment and needs to be recognized as such. As a life coach and motivational speaker, I've seen clients make progress from all different starting places by taking small steps toward an authentic goal. Sometimes seeing progress takes longer than you hoped, but it *will* happen.

TOP 1% KEY THEMES

Living in your top 1% is a continuous journey rather than a race with a start and a finish. You celebrate wins along the way and always seek out ways to improve, expand your thinking, and take on new challenges. The fun part is that your top 1% level is dynamic and constantly evolving. True top 1%ers always look for ways to raise their game and ask themselves, "Am I living up to my greatest potential?" Living in your top 1% embraces three important themes:

1. You *can* embrace a mindset that says "I can."

2. You *can* create your reality.

3. You *can* start achieving top 1% moments no matter where you are in your life.

What does an "I can" mindset look like?

MY STORY: I'm running the Los Angeles Half Marathon in two days. This race is a meaningful accomplishment because fifteen years ago I could not run more than three miles due to a cartilage tear in my left hip. I was uncertain if my injury would ever heal. I overcame the hip injury with physical therapy, stretching, and sheer determination.

Race morning at 7 a.m. is a perfect winter California day—sunshine, blue skies, and sixty-two degrees. I want to finish the race in less than two hours, even though six weeks earlier I pulled my calf in a tennis match and was unsure if it would heal in time. I feel good the morning of the race but am nervous whether or not my leg will hold up for the 13.1 miles. From the moment the race gun goes off, I keep telling myself I can do it. As I pass each mile marker, I repeat the words "I feel good." By the time I reach mile ten, I actually feel great. At mile eleven, I realize I can break two hours. At mile twelve, I realize I can achieve a personal best. I cross the finish line feeling a deep sense of fulfillment and accomplishment. Although I did not come close to winning the race or placing in my age group, I had a great experience. I used all my available physical and mental resources, including support from a friend who ran the last four miles with me, to achieve something special.

While some people aim to complete a *full* marathon, finishing a *half* marathon was a top 1% experience for me. It gave me confidence and left me with the thought, "If I can do this, what else can I accomplish?" I was so proud of myself that I hung my race medal on the inside of my front door. Every time I look at the medal it makes me smile and gives me a confidence boost. My experience of completing a half marathon can be applied to your life whether or not you like to run. A top 1% moment can include something that is a stretch or a first time achievement for you as well as something that enhances your everyday living. Running 13.1 miles may sound like an insurmountable challenge, but so will most things outside your comfort zone. You too can enjoy these moments in all of the areas that are important to you!

TAKEAWAY: Top 1% experiences are based on your personal best rather than how you do compared to others.

What does creating your reality look like?

Consider the following two examples:

BRAD'S STORY: On the East Coast, Brad was an average student with an average work ethic. His family owned a successful business, and he was expected to work in the business upon his college graduation. Brad really wanted to be an actor, but his parents did not approve. His father and five other relatives had graduated from Harvard, and he was expected to do the same. Brad knew that he was accepted into Harvard mainly due to his family alumni connections, therefore he did not feel the sense of fulfillment that comes from working hard and earning something. His life looked successful from the outside, but inside he knew that he was not on a top 1% path because he was not pursuing his dream of being an actor. Instead of tapping into what made him truly happy, Brad let his reality be created by those around him.

DANIEL'S STORY: Daniel grew up in a low-income housing development with three siblings. His dad left home when Daniel was twelve and his mom worked full-time and did her best to support the family. College was a dream rather than a reality in his family. Daniel was determined to change his future. Throughout high school he worked at a nearby restaurant and was willing to do any small job to make extra money to pay for school. He would fit his studies in early in the morning and between jobs. Despite limited financial resources, Daniel achieved great things by working hard. He was accepted into California State University, Northridge, and became the first one in his family to earn a bachelor's degree. Daniel refused to be limited by his situation and took action to create what he wanted.

TAKEAWAY: Other people can't pave the road to your top 1% — you determine the path you want to follow.

How can one achieve top 1% moments, even when they seem unattainable?

PAULA'S STORY: Meet Paula Deen, a woman who started her own business when she was forty-two years old. She had limited cooking experience, lacked a formal education, and had only $200 to spend. She created a meal delivery service called "The Bag Lady" in Savannah, Georgia. Her two sons helped her start the company by delivering meals to local businesses. People loved her cooking. Five years later, Paula took another step forward and opened her own restaurant, "The Lady and Sons." Her popularity continued to grow one success at a time as the buzz generated by her business earned her appearances on television shows such as QVC and Oprah.

Today, Paula is a best-selling author who has sold more than eight million cookbooks. The Deen brand now includes a magazine, cooking products, home goods, furniture, and a television show on the Food Network. Paula has been listed as one of *Forbes* magazine's "100 Most Influential Celebrities."

I heard Paula speak at The Women's Conference in California and was moved by her energy and her mantra, "It's *never* too late to be a success." She is excited to wake-up every morning and thinks of her life as a work in progress. She believes in doing the things "we think we can't do…starting with your thinking." Paula stepped into a life she loves by following her passion. You can too!

TAKEAWAY: You can reach your top 1% regardless of your starting place.

THE ROLE OF RITUALS

Positive energy rituals are the key to full engagement and sustained high performance.

JIM LOEHR

RITUALS DEFINED: *Conscious thoughts and actions that are consistently repeated to promote automatic behaviors and renew your energy. They help ground you, quiet your mind, and allow you to perform at your best. Rituals are the training behaviors you choose for continuous top performance.*

Positive rituals, when consistently repeated, help to train the mind and neutralize any interference that may surface. They can act as guides that will keep you on course. People who are on time, in shape, and prepared for work have one set of rituals, and people who are late, out of shape, and unprepared for work often lack a consistent set of rituals. A well-respected manager makes the time to arrive early to work, talk to his employees, and read multiple news sources to stay up-to-date with industry trends. A manager who settles for the status quo may not make it a priority during the day to check in with his employees or read the news. Both managers make choices once the alarm goes off—the top 1%ers choose behaviors that help them achieve their goals and bring them greater satisfaction. My morning ritual to focus and energize me for the day includes saying gratitude and reciting my mantra before I get out of bed, exercising, eating breakfast, and calling my mom on the East Coast.

Olympic athletes are known for using rituals, such as visualization and breathing techniques, to help them concentrate and perform in high-pressure situations. Research has shown that visualization is effective because it activates the same areas in your brain as if you completed the activity itself. Athletes train for years, yet a single two-minute routine can define their moment of glory. They have to be ready physically and mentally on the day of their event. The different rituals that elite athletes repeat help them operate at a consistently high level of excellence. Rituals can make just as much of a difference in your life.

Rituals can be practiced daily, weekly, yearly, or as often as you want. You may be familiar with rituals or traditions from a spiritual or religious practice, sorority or fraternity, or graduation ceremony. Perhaps you have a morning ritual of exercising, walking your dog, or drinking coffee. These minutes you take in the morning to clear your mind could be the foundation for the rest of your day. Many people have rituals that they practice on their birthday, anniversary, or New Year's Eve. These practices, though less frequent, may contribute to a happy family life and strengthen your relationships with the people you love.

What role do rituals play in your life? Typically, we perform simple rituals in our lives, but there are also mental rituals we can practice to condition our mind. Some people start the day with a single action such as stretching in the morning. What if you also incorporated the more expansive ritual of shifting your thoughts to create a positive mindset in everything you do? I encourage you to think bigger and broaden the concept of rituals in your life. I have intentionally used the word *rituals* because people view them as a way of life as opposed to an optional practice. The nine rituals that I will share in this book, combined with your existing best practices, will become your roadmap to living in your top 1%.

CREATING YOUR REALITY

As you begin your top 1% journey, take a few minutes to identify the differences between your *current* reality and the reality you *want* to create. Your current reality may be that your boss is a jerk, you are in an unfulfilling relationship, your job is boring, you are overweight, or you are not making as much money as you would like. These are all realities, however, they do not need to be your *permanent* reality.

Spend some time right now to think about what you want your reality to look like. Do you dream of living in a house instead of an apartment? Have you always had a desire to sing the National Anthem in a large sports stadium? Maybe you want to coach your daughter's basketball team. Is there somewhere you have always wanted to visit, and never felt you had the time? This is the time to set your ideas into action. I have yet to hear about a carpenter who built a house without any tools or someone who hit a home run without stepping up to home plate. The sooner you start to create new mental maps with the rituals that you want to follow, the sooner you will realize your full potential. It's a process, not magic.

A great way to enhance your life is by learning from the top 1%ers around you. You can begin to create the reality you want by selecting two role models who excel in many areas of their life. You could choose from friends, family members, colleagues, teachers, or anyone else who inspires you to overcome obstacles and think expansively. As you read this book and apply the nine rituals, I encourage you to reflect on the thought process and actions of the people you selected. Think about how they reach new levels of greatness. Take what you learn, then practice how you want to think and act daily. The more you practice, the sooner your behavior will become a way of life.

Many people talk about all the things they want to do, but do not follow through. Some people complain about disliking their job or having no time, yet they do not take steps to better their lives. You have to decide what you want in life and the route you will take to get there. Every person chooses his path. What route will you take?

Simply being familiar with terms such as mindset, strengths, or goals will have a limited impact in your life. The full impact will only be attained when you put these practices into action on a consistent basis. The nine rituals defined in this book will motivate you to pursue top 1% experiences and enjoy a life of happiness and fulfillment. Let's begin and find out what your top 1% looks like. You are closer than you think!

LIVING IN YOUR TOP 1%
NINE RITUALS TO ACHIEVE YOUR GOALS

RITUAL ONE: BE THE CEO OF YOU INC.
Assess YOU INC. on a continuous basis

RITUAL TWO: EMBRACE A *CAN-DO* MINDSET
Add the words "I can" to every challenge

RITUAL THREE: EXCEL WITH YOUR STRENGTHS
Identify and use your key strengths

RITUAL FOUR: GO FOR THE GOAL
Set goals annually and take one small step each day

RITUAL FIVE: THINK WITHOUT OBSTACLES
Visualize the ideal outcome

RITUAL SIX: LIVE IN YOUR STRETCH ZONE
Move outside your comfort zone

RITUAL SEVEN: DRINK A CUP OF RESILIENCE
Rise up in the face of challenges

**RITUAL EIGHT: PRACTICE THE THREE Cs:
CHOICE, COMMITMENT, AND CONSISTENCY**
Match your words and actions with your goals

RITUAL NINE: BRING BALANCE INTO YOUR LIFE
Make conscious decisions

PART 1: ASSESS

Follow your bliss and doors will open where you didn't know they were going to be.

JOSEPH CAMPBELL

BE THE CEO OF YOU INC.

To move the world, we must first move ourselves.

SOCRATES

Y OU INC. is the most important business you will ever run. When you live in your top 1%, you are the CEO, Vice President of Marketing, Sales Manager, and Human Resources Director. Your role is to oversee each of these divisions and any others that are necessary for the success of YOU INC. You make all the decisions. Regardless of where you are in your life, you can enjoy top 1% moments in all areas.

YOU INC. is similar to an investment portfolio, except it is the most significant investment you will make. Would you prefer to invest in a fund that produced below market returns or one that beat the market for the last five years? You need to diversify your portfolio and decide the proper mix of stocks, bonds, and cash. Some assets in your portfolio will outperform the market and others will underperform. Over time, you will fine-tune your investment strategy to decide the mix of securities that meets your needs.

Every asset class needs to perform to maximize your overall return. Some investors will opt for a day-trading strategy in a quest for quick profits; others will invest in mutual funds to buy and hold; and others will look for undervalued companies that can be restructured and sold for a profit. Whatever you decide to invest in, make sure that it works best for you.

Whether you are in the process of learning a new skill or hobby, moving up the corporate ladder, starting your own business, building financial security, or making time to have fun, it is important to pause and take inventory. What do you want to accomplish and are you on the right road to make it happen? You need to invest in each area of YOU INC. before you can fully give to yourself and others.

YOU INC. BLUEPRINT

Without continual growth and progress, such words as improvement, achievement, and success have no meaning.

BEN FRANKLIN

In order to make progress, you need to assess where you are vs. where you want to go. The YOU INC. blueprint creates this picture by looking at each of the key areas of your life. It gives you a snapshot of your current condition. All areas have to be working together to create the strongest, most resilient and empowered you. If you are hitting one home run after the next at work, but your relationships are strained, you are only sleeping five hours a night, and you're not eating well, can you really feel great and share your best with others?

You may notice you have a default mindset in each area. For example, in your career you may think "I can," in finances you may think "I can't," and in relationships you may think "Impossible!" When you experience wins or successes, you gain a heightened sense of confidence and a feeling that you can tackle or achieve anything. Focus on leveraging your best attitude from one area to all areas across the board. Top 1%ers continuously assess, rebalance, and set priorities in each core area of their life so they are in a position to win.

ASSESS YOU INC.

The first part in assessing YOU INC. is to identify your company's framework. What type of company do you want YOU INC. to resemble? Although you may not consider yourself a "company," your life is made up of different areas just like the best corporations. Do you want YOU INC. to be innovative like Apple, produce consistent returns like GE, or provide entertainment value like Disney? Think of your role models or the two people you selected in the prior section. What kind of "company" do they run? What aspects of each person do you admire? This assessment can be a good starting point to understand what you want.

Take a moment and look at the YOU INC. blueprint on the next page. The five questions and exercises listed after the blueprint will help you gain clarity in each area. I encourage you to take a few minutes right now to reflect as you work through these exercises. They will form the foundation for your personal roadmap which will lead you to live in your top 1%. You can use the *IDEAS* page at the end of this ritual to write down your responses.

This assessment process is a powerful method to keep you progressing toward your top performance. This exercise should be done at least once a year, but can be adjusted more frequently when helpful. Life's unexpected changes can bring about a need to restructure YOU INC. at any given time. These adjustments will become easy to make after enough practice. Just as successful companies constantly adjust to meet current trends and market demands, so will you when managing YOU INC.

YOU INC. BLUEPRINT

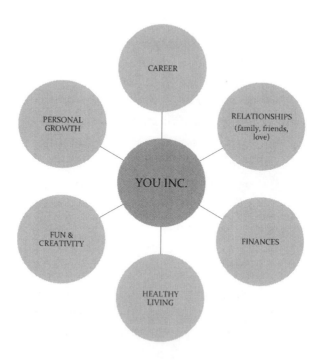

© ALISSA FINERMAN

1. **Identify the core areas in your personal YOU INC. blueprint.**

In the YOU INC. blueprint, there are six separate areas. You may want to change or add an area to more accurately represent your best self. For example, one client renamed the *Personal Growth* area *Go Beyond Limits* because it had greater meaning to him. Start by breaking down the whole and examining each part. If you bought a business, you would evaluate it by focusing on each separate area, including sales, marketing, and finance. Use the same process for yourself.

2. **Rate each area on a scale of 1 to 10 based on where you are today (10 being the highest rating, meaning you are 100% fulfilled and satisfied with that area of your life).**

Without being judgmental about what you have or have not accomplished in each area, take a few minutes to reflect and be honest with yourself. Too many people focus on what's wrong or what they are not doing. This process gives you the opportunity to start fresh. If you want to improve something, this is your chance. If you rated an area a 7, think about what the gap from a 7 to a 10 represents. What would a 10 look like?

I did a similar assessment for the first time in 2005, and it helped to clarify which areas of my life I was making strides in and which areas needed additional attention. Five years later, I looked at this entry in my journal and found it interesting to compare areas and observe changes. I experienced dramatic shifts upward in *Work* and *Fun & Creativity*; the *Work* area went from a 5 to an 8 and the *Fun & Creativity* area increased from a 4 to a 7. I continue to focus on these and other areas in the blueprint, specifically *Career* and *Relationships*.

3. List as many wins as you can for each area.

A win is when you take a positive step forward and feel good about what you have accomplished. If you are pursuing a new hobby, and recently browsed the course catalog or signed up for a class those would be considered wins. If you are trying to take better care of yourself, and exercised for thirty minutes or went to sleep before midnight for the past week those would count as wins. Whether you rated an area a 1 or a 10, there has to be at least one positive thing you've accomplished. Although you may be tempted to remind yourself of the areas where you are weakest, this exercise is about starting to condition your mind to think what you *can* do. Even the smallest win should make you feel good about yourself.

4. Which areas are assets and which ones are liabilities that drain your energy?

This step is simply to assess and take note of what's working and what you might consider doing differently. What are your best assets? Are you leveraging your assets to have the greatest impact? What common themes can you extract from your successes? Your time and energy are precious resources, so you must invest them appropriately. Areas that are top priorities require your best thinking and actions.

5. What steps can you take to move into your top 1% in each area?

For now, please list any thoughts on the *IDEAS* page. You can refine them as you move through the book. If you want to increase the *Fun & Creativity* area and take a vacation, you might decide to assess your spending habits for the month and start saving $50 a week. If you want to build your business by getting ten new clients, you can join two networking groups, attend an industry conference, and build brand awareness through online social media platforms.

> **TOP 1% TIP:** *Personalize the YOU INC. blueprint by adding your initials or using words that inspire you. For example, you could rename it "CKF INC." or "MY YEAR OF SUCCESS."*

MAKE YOURSELF A PRIORITY

Top 1% living starts with you. It is about putting yourself in a position to win and making decisions that bring out your best. When you're at your best, you can more freely give your best to others. Although you may have multiple priorities, managing YOU INC. must be a core focus. If you constantly feel overwhelmed, pulled in multiple directions, drained, and deprived of time for yourself, adopting this ritual is essential.

Are YOU a priority?

In order to effectively run and manage YOU INC., you need to start with the belief that it is okay to make yourself a priority. To be your best, you need to take care of YOU INC. across the board. Band-Aid remedies will only take you so far.

Answer these five true-or-false statements to assess the current priority of YOU INC.

1. T/F: You make time for yourself every day.

2. T/F: You do one positive thing for yourself daily.

3. T/F: Your most important asset is YOU.

4. T/F: You feel fulfilled and energized, as opposed to guilty, when you do something for yourself.

5. T/F: You consider the needs of others and your needs when figuring out solutions.

Let's make sense of your responses:

Five true—If you answered "true" to every question, you are a master at making yourself a priority.

Question to consider: How effective are you at balancing your needs with the needs of the important people in your life?

Four true—If you answered "true" to four questions, you are highly effective at making yourself a priority.

Question to consider: What actions could you take, if any, to make yourself a top priority?

Three true—If you answered "true" to three questions, you sometimes make yourself a priority and frequently put others ahead of you.

Question to consider: What impact would it have on your life to make yourself a higher priority?

Zero - two true—If you answered "true" to zero, one, or two questions, you should use this as a wake-up call to think of how you can make yourself a priority.

If you do not make yourself a priority, who will?

We all have priorities in our lives such as family, work, relationships, and health. No matter what our individual priorities are, time demands exist that pull us in every direction. The challenge is to make yourself a priority. Often we spend hours on others and ignore our own needs. When you fly, and the flight attendants share safety/emergency tips, they advise you to put your oxygen mask on first before you help others. Without giving yourself oxygen you can't survive, and are therefore unable to care for others. Making yourself a priority is the process of fueling yourself.

Is it really possible to prioritize yourself when you have a busy life and other pressures? Absolutely! Once you realize that your needs are non-negotiable, you will accomplish more.

How do you make yourself a priority when you're married, have young children, and have a business to run?

ALLISON'S STORY: My client Allison was a busy small business owner who struggled to make time for herself during the day. Between taking her children to school in the morning and then picking them up three hours later, she felt like there was no time in the day just for her. She worked from home, so it was difficult to separate work from taking care of the children. She wanted to grow her business, but barely had enough time to work on projects, let alone get new clients. Money was tight, so hiring help was not an alternative. We evaluated options and focused on how to free up her time.

Allison decided that she needed one additional hour a day to allow for personal time and to develop her business. The extra time would enable her to exercise several times a week, make progress on her work projects, and have one business lunch a week. Thinking creatively, she talked to the neighbors on her block and set up a babysitting sharing and carpool program.

As a result, Allison created five hours of free time per week. After two months she had generated two new clients and had enough money to hire part-time help. Most importantly, the extra time gave her space to think and be proactive about her life and her business, rather than reactive to emails and phone calls all day long.

TAKEAWAY: *You can make yourself a priority by making a few small adjustments to your daily routine.*

Sometimes making yourself a priority can seem overwhelming. It's best to start the process by doing one small thing a day and seeing what you can handle. Small steps could include spending one minute to say gratitude, focusing for five minutes to schedule your daily priorities, taking ten minutes to read or meditate, carving out fifteen minutes to connect with a good friend on the phone, exercising for thirty minutes, or simply thinking of your needs in a specific situation. You can do something good for yourself in less than ten minutes.

Are you like some people who make themselves a priority less often than they would like? Do not feel bad; it's an easy habit to fall into. We are used to showing up for others, yet we think it is optional to show up for ourselves. Would you think it's optional to care for your dog or a young child? Even cars get serviced regularly and refueled. We tend to think that carving out time for ourselves is selfish. The truth is, when you feel good, you have more to give to others. Making YOU INC. a priority is non-negotiable, rather than optional. You might even enjoy putting yourself first.

TOP 1% TIP: *Make a list of seven ways that you can make yourself a priority. Each item on the list should be doable in less than fifteen minutes. For the next week, complete one item a day and check it off the list. Ideas include: reading a magazine you enjoy, listening to your favorite song to unwind, organizing the "junk" drawer that you've been meaning to clean out for months, or treating yourself to a fifteen-minute massage.*

MANAGING YOU INC. IS A BALANCING ACT

Making yourself a priority does not have to be an all or nothing game. Some may say, "I do not have time for myself." Others may have the time, but feel guilty when they put themselves first. It is difficult to make your needs a priority when family and work are involved. Despite the fact that it is challenging, remember that it is possible.

CONFLICT: You have a major customer presentation that you've been trying to schedule for six months. Your brother is taking a four-day vacation for his anniversary and he asks you to watch his two young kids. The presentation is Monday and you need to spend the entire weekend with the kids, leaving you little time to prepare. You are very busy at work, and the weekend is the only time you have. If the meeting goes well, it's likely you will get the promotion you have been focusing on for the past six months. Since multiple parties are involved, it would be difficult to postpone or cancel the meeting.

QUESTION: Do you cancel everything on your schedule and disregard your priorities to help your brother or do you get creative and figure out solutions?

VALUES AND PRIORITIES: You value both family and your career. Your priorities are to help your brother so he can celebrate his anniversary and to win the customer business so you can advance your career.

SOLUTION: You figure out a workable solution that includes preparing during the weeknights for the presentation, getting a babysitter for a few hours on Saturday, and asking your brother to take an earlier flight back on Sunday to give you time to prepare.

FINE-TUNE YOUR EXISTING RITUALS

Take a moment and consider the rituals you currently embrace to see if they are adding value and producing results. Remember, rituals are the consistent mental and physical practices that help you excel and perform at your highest level. Are your daily practices enhancing or detracting from your happiness? How do they contribute to YOU INC.? If the rituals get in the way of your growth then a tune-up is in order. Often, a small and simple shift in a ritual in one area of your life can make a big difference in another area.

PATRICK'S STORY: A client, Patrick, was in the middle of a divorce and found it difficult to be at his best when he saw his soon-to-be ex-wife. These run-ins left him upset for several hours and he found it challenging to think clearly. Patrick had a ritual of exercising four mornings a week at the gym before going to the office. Although in the past this was a positive ritual, it now detracted from Patrick's day because his ex-wife lived on the same block as his gym. As a result, he frequently bumped into her on the way to his car.

After discussing the conflict, we clarified that while in the past his morning ritual added value to his day it now had a negative effect on his mental well-being and prevented him from being his best. He was resistant to change because he felt comfortable at this gym and enjoyed seeing his friends there. I suggested that he try going to a different gym location for one week. The week passed and he did not bump into his ex-wife. As a result, his stress level decreased and he felt energized after his workout. Patrick still had to deal with the emotional stress of the divorce, but this small change in his daily ritual helped to refuel him for the day as it previously had.

TAKEAWAY: Only repeat rituals that enhance YOU INC. and add value to your day.

BOTTOM LINE SUMMARY

RITUAL ONE: BE THE CEO OF YOU INC.
Assess YOU INC. on a continuous basis

You have the potential to make YOU INC. a very successful company. The market is untapped and waiting for you to get involved. There is a tremendous opportunity for personal growth. You can lead YOU INC. in whatever direction you choose. As you move through the book, determine which of the current rituals that you already practice enhance YOU INC. and which ones detract from your goals. This is the time for YOU INC. to thrive.

KEY PRACTICES TO HELP YOU EMBRACE THIS RITUAL

1. Step into the CEO role of YOU INC. Remember that you are in control of all operations.

2. Make yourself a priority and focus on your greatest asset— you.

3. Focus on choices that enhance YOU INC. and help to redefine your potential.

TOP 1% PEP TALK
You've taken the hardest step, which is to begin to assess and generate ideas about your priorities. If you are feeling overwhelmed, intimidated, or unsure if you can do this, please know that you are not alone. Stay with it and take one small step at a time. Each win will give you energy to continue.

IDEAS

_____

_____

_____

_____

_____

_____

_____

_____

_____

_____

RITUAL TWO

EMBRACE A *CAN-DO* MINDSET

As a single footstep will not make a path on the earth, so a single thought will not make a pathway in the mind. To make a deep physical path, we walk again and again. To make a deep mental path, we must think over and over the kind of thoughts we wish to dominate our lives.

HENRY DAVID THOREAU

You never know when you will be called upon to produce your top 1%. There is no reason to wait until you have a crisis or are faced with a serious health issue. You need to know who you are and where you stand. External events can rattle the ground beneath you, but when you are clear on your values and beliefs, you will stay grounded throughout the storm. My advice—shift your mindset today to say "I can" and prepare yourself for all your tomorrows.

> **MINDSET DEFINED:** *Mindset is a set of beliefs that define who you are and what you can do. This set of beliefs defines what is possible and what is impossible.*

According to the National Science Foundation, our brains can produce as many as 50,000 thoughts per day. Ninety-five percent of these thoughts are repeated daily. You decide how you think and what becomes a *can* or *can't*. Your thoughts become your beliefs which, in turn, become your mindset. Your mindset governs your actions, which make up your reality. The following chain reaction illustrates the effect that your thoughts can have on your life.

Thoughts » Beliefs » Belief System » Mindset » Actions » Reality

When you repeat the same thought often enough, it becomes your belief. You have beliefs about yourself at work, at home, in relationships, and in all other areas of your life. In your career, you may have a *can-do* belief, but with your finances you may feel helpless and fail to apply the same beliefs that help you excel elsewhere. These beliefs may vary in each area and depend on past successes and your ability to overcome challenges. The goal is to be aware of your thoughts so that you can turn them into positive beliefs.

Your individual beliefs are similar to chapters in a book. When you put them all together, you have the belief system that becomes your own story. The more you repeat your story, the more you believe it. The more you believe it, the more you become it. Therefore, your belief system is the catalyst for all that you do.

Carol Dweck, a psychologist at Stanford University and author of *Mindset*, has researched achievement and success for twenty years and has found that these life stories, which we create from our beliefs, will either enhance or undermine our life goals. People often use stories to explain their situations and to make excuses for leaving them unchanged. Although we all have difficult stories to tell, the key is not to let these stories prevent us from making progress.

If you continue to doubt every move you make and tell yourself "I can't" day after day, the chances that you *can't* and you *won't* increase dramatically. If you say "I'll never get promoted" or "I can't date any good guys," these beliefs become your story. If you repeatedly tell people a story about your inability to get promoted, you will own that story. It is just as easy to own a more positive story that will help you realize your goals and achieve greater fulfillment. Both take effort to repeat to the world. Top 1%ers tell a story that says "I can." As you share these beliefs and stories, they become hard-wired into your brain to form your mindset.

Your mindset can be as powerful or as destructive as you make it. Dweck believes that people who have a desire to learn and improve each day reach higher levels of achievement. Her research shows that a growth mindset will take you further than a fixed mindset. Do you have a growth mindset? Which beliefs below reflect how you think more frequently?

FIXED MINDSET	GROWTH MINDSET ✓
"Golf is not my game."	"If at first you don't succeed, try, try again."
"If I don't get the job, it wasn't meant to happen."	"Rome wasn't built in a day."
"The hand you are dealt is the one you own."	"Your true potential is unlimited."

TOP 1% TIP: *Think about a phrase you say frequently that reinforces a negative belief and reword it in a positive way. Instead of repeating the words, "My house is a mess," try saying something more productive such as, "I want a clutter-free home." You can use the IDEAS page to jot down new phrases you want to use.*

MY STORY: When I started on the corporate bond sales desk, I had a few small accounts that rarely did a trade. On the rare occasion my accounts did a trade, it was typically small and the trading desk did not care because they would not make money on it. I was frustrated not to have any big accounts and be involved in the day-to-day trading flow. This made for a long day. All the traders continually told me how challenging it would be to build my account base. I was ready for the challenge.

I repeatedly told myself I would get in the trading game soon. The only way to achieve this goal was to build one of my customers into an active trading account. I had one hedge fund that had the potential to be a large customer. There were two traders that worked at the account. One was easy to work with and the other was difficult to handle. The challenging one was your best friend one day and screaming at you the next. Each phone call was a new surprise. My trading desk did not trust them, which made it difficult to have a strong relationship. Regardless of the complications, I knew this account was the key to success in my job. I simply told myself I could turn this customer into a top account on the desk and then made it happen. I only thought about being successful. I never considered a different alternative.

This hedge fund was my main focus every single day for the entire year. I treated the account like gold. I spoke to the two traders every morning before 7.30 a.m. to give them a market update and touched base with them at least ten times throughout the day. They were my first call whenever we had a new deal or trade idea. I visited the two traders at the account and slowly built a relationship with them. We played tennis several times after work, had business dinners with the traders on my desk, and saw a U2 concert at Madison Square Garden. I invested a lot of time and energy to build this relationship and my career.

At the end of the year, I traded over $5 billion with the account and had established myself on the corporate bond trading desk. I gained confidence from the win and was ready to take on a new challenge. This journey was possible because I had a *can-do* mindset.

TAKEAWAY: A focused and determined mindset will dictate how you view challenges and what you can and can't achieve.

BELIEFS OF THE TOP 1%

People become really quite remarkable when they start thinking that they can do things. When they believe in themselves they have the first secret of success.

NORMAN VINCENT PEALE

People who possess a top 1% mindset are open to new challenges. They stretch themselves and find new opportunities to learn and grow. You can define what excellence means to you. It is not a competition, so start where you are and take one small step at a time. Start asking if you are putting yourself in a position to win. If not, learn from your past experiences and make new choices.

Begin to incorporate the following beliefs into your mindset as you continue on your journey:

- I choose words that are positive and supportive.
- I make choices that enhance YOU INC.
- I use words that create a powerful mindset.
- I think without limits.
- I can create my ideal lifestyle.

DAWN'S STORY: Dawn graduated from the University of Southern California and decided to take an entry-level job as a receptionist at a residential real estate company in Los Angeles. She was unsure about a career choice. What she did know was that she wanted to be independent and have flexibility during the day. She was interested in real estate and thought she would enjoy the challenge of building relationships and negotiating transactions.

After being exposed to the culture, Dawn decided to explore a career in residential real estate. The brokers in her firm told her it was a difficult time to start in the business and blatantly tried to dissuade her from trying. She believed in herself and did not let the discouragement deter her. Twelve months later she received her real estate license and, within three years, became a top producer in her office. The amazing part of the story is that Dawn was the first one in her family to graduate from college and earn a six-figure income. Most importantly, she now loves her workday and has the freedom to make her own schedule. She continues to redefine her top 1% level.

TAKEAWAY: *Your starting point determines where you begin. You determine where you finish.*

MINDSET MAKES A DIFFERENCE

Whether you think you can, or think you can't, you are right.

HENRY FORD

As a child you are taught certain beliefs, by both the media and society. These beliefs will continue to be challenged and shaped throughout your life. The difference between *good* and *great* is grounded in what you believe you can achieve. When you tell yourself you can't do something, you will be right. It is unproductive to embrace negative thoughts.

Barbara Fredrickson, a positive psychologist and author of *Positivity*, shows through her research that positivity can change how your mind works. "Positivity doesn't just change the contents of your mind, trading bad thoughts for good ones; it also changes the scope or boundaries of your mind. It widens the span of possibilities that you see." Most people have a 2:1 ratio of positive to negative emotions. Barbara discusses the importance of experiencing at least a 3:1 positivity ratio in order to be more resilient and flourish. At this new level she points out, "a transformation occurs. You feel more alive, creative and resilient...this is flourishing." It takes three positive comments to neutralize one negative one. The good news is you can construct the mindset that is best for you.

WHAT'S YOUR MINDSET?

One of the main weaknesses of mankind is the average
person's familiarity with the word 'impossible.'
He knows all the rules that will not work.
He knows all the things that cannot be done.

NAPOLEON HILL

Do you have a *can-do*, resilient mindset, or a negative mindset that makes you unwilling to cope with challenges? A positive mindset helps you make progress. A self-limiting mindset prevents you from reaching your "A" game. One way to determine the type of mindset you embrace is by examining the way you interpret different situations. Read the five statements below and choose the response that you would most likely have in each of the scenarios.

1. You have your performance review at work and your boss shares both positive and negative feedback with you.

    A. You are upset that your boss focuses on the negative areas and disagree with his assessment.

    B. You have a productive conversation with your boss and steer the conversation to focus on how to improve the weaker areas that matter.

2. You share a business plan with several investors who do not think your plan will be successful.

    A. You start to doubt your idea and consider bailing on the concept.

    B. You thank them for their feedback, fine-tune the plan, and talk to other investors. You continue to believe in yourself.

3. You start playing golf at the age of 45 and feel frustrated because you can't score below one hundred.

    A. You say, "I hate golf," and throw your clubs in the closet. "I'll never be good at this sport."

    B. You sign up for a golf clinic and start working on key areas of your game to improve.

4. You find out that your partner of five years cheated on you with one of your friends.

    A. You start thinking about what you did wrong to cause this situation and feel like you are never going to fall in love again.

    B. You feel deeply hurt but realize that you deserve friends and lovers who are faithful. You take time for yourself and reach out to your support system to help you move forward.

5. A friend compliments your outfit and tells you how great you look.

    A. You doubt she means the compliment and try to downplay it by telling her you look thinner because you are wearing all black.

    B. You accept the compliment and say, "Thank you!" You tell her you've been working out and appreciate her noticing.

The "A" responses represent a negative, self-doubting mindset, and the "B" responses represent a hopeful, confident and *can-do* mindset. Do your natural responses lean toward A or B? Your responses may be a mixture of A and B. Try not to judge yourself. Reflect on the assessment and think about your role models and the two people you selected who may have a mindset you admire. What do you like about the words they use in different types of situations? Whether you are closer to a *can-do* mindset or a self-doubting mindset, decide right now to make progress toward the mindset you desire.

> **TOP 1% TIP:** *Try this for one month: Put $1 in a jar or envelope every time you say a negative word or phrase such as "I can't" or "Today is a disaster." Share your intentions with a few friends and ask them to hold you accountable. At the end of the month, see how much you have raised and turn those negative dollars into something positive by donating them to your favorite charity. This is also a great exercise for managers to practice around the office to keep employees thinking positively.*

CONDITION YOUR MIND

To reach a top 1% thinking state, you have to have a regimen that helps you think freely in order to generate great ideas. My favorite ways to create this positive environment include hiking in the Santa Monica Mountains, reading, and running on the beach. You may prefer to meditate, listen to music, write, or do another activity that puts you in what some refer to as *flow*. This concept is described by Mihaly Csikszentmihalyi, author of the book *Flow: The Psychology of Optimal Experience*, as "being completely involved in an activity for its own sake. The ego falls away. Time flies. Every action, movement, and thought follows inevitably from the previous one. Your whole being is involved, and you are using your skills to the utmost." You will find yourself in flow when the skills necessary for the task are high enough to meet the challenge. You are in flow when you are fully immersed, absorbed, and engaged in an activity.

Top 1% thinking only happens with a clear, focused, and calm mind. You do not attach yourself to any single thought or get lost in the details. You are focused on the bigger picture and how to get there. Building a positive mindset is the process of quieting the distractions or "noise" in your head so you can think in your top 1%. If you want a certain result, you will have to have a specific set of beliefs, rituals, and actions.

SUSAN'S STORY: Susan, a forty-five-year-old advertising manager, was negative about everything when we started our coaching sessions. She was an intelligent woman who held a lot of responsibility at work, but was surprisingly unaware of the effect of her thoughts. Her mindset was limiting her ability to advance in the company.

The company brought me in to work with her. I asked her to keep a journal of her thoughts for one day without judging herself. It was an exercise to help her see the balance of negative to positive thoughts. She tracked her reactions to clients, co-workers, and her family.

The next time we met, she was amazed that her mind naturally found the negative in every situation. Almost *all* of her reactions were negative. We determined there was a mismatch between the thoughts she had and how she wanted to be viewed at work. She needed to change her inputs if she wanted different results. She evaluated her thoughts and communication style with co-workers to improve her image and the transformation started.

Within three weeks, she received positive feedback from her co-workers about her shift in mindset and was asked to lead a key project. She even noticed that her husband wanted to spend more time with her. It is possible to change your inputs and get different results quickly. This major win was accomplished in a short period of time because Susan took the time and effort to bring awareness to her thoughts and had the courage to change them.

TAKEAWAY: The first step toward shifting your mindset is to be honest with yourself and recognize if your thoughts tend to be positive or negative.

Take a moment and think about the words you use the majority of the time. Do they empower you or limit your potential? How often do you use the words "I can't" vs. "I can"? When you are ready to change your words, you will be on the path to seeing different results. The goal is to assess your words without judgment and to start using the words that will help you build a resilient mindset. *Change your words, change your life.*

SAY GOODBYE TO SELF-LIMITING BELIEFS

We all have self-limiting beliefs and doubts. People tend to limit themselves without good reason. They often do not try to reach their highest potential for fear of failure. If you have never started a business, it does not follow that you can't do it. Similarly, if you have no experience as a salesperson, it does not mean sales is not for you. Top 1%ers refrain from drawing conclusions based on insufficient information or one piece of information. They identify these beliefs, negate them, and then move forward.

You *can* reduce your negative self-talk. You begin by becoming aware of how you are talking. The next step is to dispute the irrational belief immediately. You need to decipher if the belief is temporary and can be modified, or permanent and cannot be modified. Few beliefs are truly permanent.

It is your choice how you analyze a chain of events. Take the following two options for example:

Option 1: A) You start a business » B) Business fails » *C) You are a failure.*

Option 2: A) You start a business » B) Business fails » *C) You are one step closer to creating your next successful business.*

The effective way to interpret the above situation is to stick to the facts and stay objective, as in Option 2. You started a business that was a good idea, yet the business did not succeed. The conclusion, part C, is your choice.

What is important is how you piece together the facts leading to the failure and what your takeaways are as you learn from each experience. Overly negative and dramatic comments are unproductive and can drain your energy. Failure is simply feedback on what to do differently next time. Use it to create the story you want to embody. *Winners use winning words.*

TOP 1% TIP: Pick an area in the YOU INC. blueprint that you want to improve. Create a phrase that empowers you and reinforces what you want to bring into your life. Commit to repeating this mantra first thing in the morning for the next month. Choose a mantra that resonates with you and believe it when you say it. You will notice how repeating a few simple words can set a positive tone for the day. Examples of mantras include: "I deserve to be treated with respect," "I am strong and healthy," or "I bring loving relationships into my life."

SPRING-CLEANING TIME

To create your winning mindset, you will have to do some spring-cleaning and throw out words and phrases that no longer serve your vision. It will take effort and awareness to condition your mind for peak performance. An effective way to condition your mind is to stretch it and do new things. If Google, eBay, and Coca-Cola did everything the same way year after year, they would become stagnant. YOU INC. also needs stimulation to evolve. Thinking the same way and expecting different results is unrealistic. In order to grow, you will need to exercise and expand your thinking.

A patient recovering from surgery can have a daily mantra either saying, "I feel great and am getting stronger every day," or "It's going to take me forever to get better." The words are his or her choice. Top 1%ers choose a positive mantra. If you want better results, you too must choose to condition your mind accordingly.

OLD MINDSET (I can't)	NEW MINDSET (I can) √
I have the worst luck.	I work hard and create my own luck.
Everyone has limits.	The possibilities are limitless.
I do not have enough time.	I make time for my priorities.

Your words are your choice and they have the power to enable dramatically different results. Think about the words you would use if you had to develop a marketing campaign for YOU INC. Nike used the tagline, "Just Do It," to inspire millions. What tagline would best represent your brand and mindset?

BOTTOM LINE SUMMARY

RITUAL TWO: EMBRACE A *CAN-DO* MINDSET
Add the words "I can" to each challenge

If you do not like something, change it. If you can't change it, change your attitude.

MAYA ANGELOU

Top 1%ers possess a *can-do* mindset which instills hope and creates opportunities. On a day-to-day basis, start to notice the words you choose and the beliefs you live by. Your words are like hearing your favorite song on the radio. You can either hear the song *I can't* one hundred times a day or *I can*. Just as you get to decide which radio station to listen to, you have the choice of which lyrics run through your mind. You will enjoy more top 1% moments when you start applying your best thinking from one area to everything you do.

At one time, people thought it was impossible to run a mile in under four minutes. It was impossible until 1954 when Roger Bannister ran the first sub-four-minute mile in three minutes and 59.4 seconds. Running a mile in under four minutes has since become the standard rather than the exception for professional runners. In fact, even high school runners have broken this barrier. Roger's accomplishment helped other runners expand their beliefs of what is possible. The next time you step onto your playing field of choice—whether it is a boardroom, tennis court, or family dinner—take a moment to pause and listen to the thoughts running through your mind. Put yourself in an inspiring environment and surround yourself with positive people that help you reach new levels.

KEY PRACTICES TO HELP YOU EMBRACE THIS RITUAL

1. Focus on using the words "I can."

2. Create the story that empowers you.

3. Take control of your Thoughts » Beliefs » Belief System » Mindset » Actions » Reality.

TOP 1% PEP TALK

Congratulations on completing the second ritual. You've made it through the challenging part. Keep taking one step at a time, and I promise you will end up with a big result. Next, we focus on strengths. Let's keep rolling!

IDEAS

RITUAL THREE

EXCEL WITH YOUR STRENGTHS

Success is achieved by developing our strengths, not by eliminating our weaknesses.

MARILYN VOS SAVANT

Your strengths are your differentiators. Everyone has their own personal set. They are what make you "you." Top 1%ers combine their strengths to deliver their best. The challenge is to identify these strengths, use them daily, and put them into action.

As you read through this section, focus on gaining clarity on the following questions:

1. What are your strengths?

2. How effectively do you use your strengths daily?

3. What can you do to use your strengths in all areas of YOU INC.?

What would your co-workers, friends, or spouse say are your top strengths? My strengths as a coach are encouraging clients to think beyond obstacles, redefining their potential, and designing empowering goals. Your strengths as a friend may include being patient, supportive, and a great listener. In your career, you might be effective at negotiating, building trust, and bringing clarity to complex projects. Focusing on your strengths will help you shine and reinforce the things you *can* do.

The Gallup Organization has spent several decades studying how people can be their best every day. It surveyed more than ten million people across cultures, industries, and positions to learn about their strengths. Their research has shown that a strengths-based approach improves things such as confidence, direction, and hope. People who use their strengths and focus on them every day are "six times as likely to be engaged in their jobs and more than three times as likely to report having an excellent quality of life in general." The research uncovered that at least seven million people fall short of reaching their highest level. Some people do not know their strengths and others do not effectively use them.

The idea of using your strengths to live a happier life is also encouraged in the field of positive psychology. This new branch of psychology, started in 1998, is the study of what makes people flourish and lead more fulfilling lives. This is a novel approach, because psychology in the past focused on what was *wrong* with people. Dr. Martin Seligman, considered to be the "father of positive psychology," has shown through his research that happiness, fulfillment, and satisfaction levels can be increased regardless of one's situation. To reach higher and more fulfilling levels of happiness, he highlights the importance of focusing on character strengths or traits such as kindness, zest, gratitude, and love of learning. Our strengths are not limited to qualities that can be applied in the workplace; they include all of the things that make us shine as unique individuals and differentiate us from one another.

STRENGTHS MAKE A DIFFERENCE

When you use your strengths effectively, they pull you in an upward spiral and lead to feelings of hope, optimism, contentment, and gratitude. Positive psychologist Barbara Fredrickson created the *Broaden-and-Build Theory* to shed light on the Theory of Positive Emotions. She explains the impact of positive emotions: "They open our hearts and our minds, making us more receptive and more creative," and "they allow us to discover and build new skills, new ties, new knowledge, and new ways of being." Her research shows that positivity helps people thrive and become their best.

KRISTEN'S STORY: My fifty-year-old client Kristen, a finance manager in a retail company, was bored, had low energy, and was not engaged at work or in her relationships. I encouraged her to spend twenty minutes to take a *strengths assessment*. Her top strengths were gratitude, love of learning, and creativity. She noticed that she was not using her strengths on a daily basis at work, home, or in her relationships. This was the first time she ever made this realization.

I wanted Kristen to make some progress and build confidence before she addressed her work situation. I believed she could make an immediate impact in her personal life, so I encouraged her to think about her ideal Saturday, using her strengths to get her moving. She was excited. She envisioned a beautiful

Saturday that included writing in the morning, counseling teens at a local nonprofit, reading in the afternoon, and having dinner with friends.

Over the next month, she took steps to put parts of her ideal Saturday in place. She volunteered to counsel teens once a month, signed up for a creative writing class, and organized a dinner party to let her friends know how grateful she was to have them in her life. An amazing thing happened—she made a few small changes to her Saturday and felt like a new person. She had something to look forward to and was doing the activities she enjoyed.

After improving her Saturdays and feeling the benefits, she felt confident enough to talk to her boss about changing roles within the company. Her journey started because we identified her strengths and applied them in a meaningful way. Progress is about being proactive and creating what you desire.

TAKEAWAY: Taking the time to identify your strengths will present a clearer path forward.

IDENTIFY YOUR STRENGTHS

Some people have trouble identifying their strengths. If you do not consistently remind yourself of your best qualities, you tend to forget what they are. The following section provides you with four effective ways to gain insights about your specific strengths. Many of my clients have made significant improvements in their lives by completing some or all of the following assessments. To get the most well rounded picture of your strengths, I encourage you to do as many of these assessments as you can. Each option offers unique and valuable insights and may provide you with a new perspective.

1. **VIA SURVEY OF CHARACTER STRENGTHS:** Visit www.authentichappiness.com and take the VIA Survey of Character Strengths developed by Martin Seligman and Chris Peterson with support from the VIA Institute.

This is a free online assessment with 240-questions and it will take twenty minutes to complete. The survey results will list your top five strengths and rank your complete list of twenty-four strengths. The purpose of taking this assessment is to identify and validate your strengths and determine how you can incorporate these strengths on a daily basis.

2. **STRENGTHSFINDER:** Visit www.strengthsfinder.com and take the assessment.

The assessment gives you insight on your top five themes, a strengths discovery activity, and a strengths-based action plan. Tom Rath and the Gallup scientists created this online assessment after studying millions of people. You will need an access code to register which is provided in the inside back cover of *StrengthsFinder 2.0*, by Tom Rath.

3. **BEST SELF EXERCISE:** Assess your strengths with the Reflected Best Self Exercise, developed by the Center for Positive Organizational Scholarship at the University of Michigan's Ross School of Business.

This four-step approach is more time intensive but will give you a personal way of recognizing your strengths and the opportunity to reconnect with important people in your life. First, you identify and contact between ten and twenty people who you trust to offer thoughtful input. They can be co-workers, friends, customers, or family members. Next, you create a feedback form to distribute to your group. You ask each person to share three stories about you at your best and how you add value in different situations. In the third and fourth steps, you analyze the feedback, extract common themes, and create one master "Best Self."

If you are open to making yourself vulnerable to a wider audience and have the time, this is an effective option. This approach was featured in the *Harvard Business Review*.

4. STRENGTHS ASSESSMENT 101: Ask ten people to identify your top three strengths.

This method is a fun and interactive way to gain insights about your strengths from the people you interact with on a regular basis. The ten people you select should be a mixture of people from different areas of your life such as colleagues, friends, managers, teachers, and coaches whose opinion you value and trust. Invite them to share your key strengths that help you excel and bring out your best. Bring the common themes together, see what you agree with, and then reflect to see if you are using these strengths on a daily basis. Often, it is helpful to gain feedback from good friends or people who know you well. The insights can be enlightening.

Each exercise will help you gain valuable insights about your strengths and provide you with a base assessment. Give yourself time to reflect on the feedback and see if you agree with the results. Occasionally, you may not agree with one of the top findings—that's okay. Some will be more obvious than others. Think about whether or not you are using these strengths on a daily basis at work, in relationships, and in new situations.

Recognizing what your true strengths are provides a temporary boost to your confidence. It's a good feeling to have your strengths validated. Using your strengths will lead to a greater sense of accomplishment and fulfillment.

> **TOP 1% TIP:** *Choose three of your top strengths and write down how you can apply each of these strengths to the different areas in the YOU INC. blueprint. You will notice that your strongest qualities can be useful across the board.*

USE YOUR STRENGTHS TO OVERCOME CHALLENGES

Life comes at you from all different angles. Some days are great and everything flows in your favor, and other days are a struggle and you can't wait for the day to be over. Regardless of the externality of the situation and what is going on around you, you always have your strengths to depend on. Whether or not it is a sunny or rainy day, you are the same on the inside. Whether you are facing a new challenge at work or at home, you still own your strengths. Top 1%ers are particularly effective at applying their strengths to overcome challenging situations.

TIM'S STORY: My client Tim, a thirty-eight-year-old marketing manager was doing great in his job and as a result was given greater responsibility. He eventually left to start his own firm. Tim struggled more than he expected when he ventured out on his own. The pressure to get new clients and hire new talent was overwhelming. It was not the same environment. Starting a new firm was tough and required time to execute a business plan and build a client base. Tim was pushed so far outside his comfort zone that he was not thinking clearly. He needed to be reminded of his strengths and how to use them.

After three coaching sessions, Tim developed an action plan to apply his top strengths which included leadership, humor, and determination. He got his confidence back and started to set priorities for himself and the business. He lightened up the stressful mood in the office with his humor and shared his compelling vision for the business with his employees. He then posted his action plan in the conference room to motivate his team. Tim still had challenges to face, but he was once again operating at his top level by using his strengths.

The result: Tim built a profitable firm, and within eighteen months had twelve new clients and hired three additional employees.

> TAKEAWAY: It's easy to lose sight of your strengths in difficult times. Remembering what they are and how to use them will help you get back on track.

ONLY ADDRESS WEAKNESSES THAT MATTER

Top 1%ers are aware of their weaker areas and allocate time to improve the ones they deem most important. It is okay to have weaknesses and not to be on top of your game every day. We all have various areas that are weak, but trying to address them all would both take up the majority of our time and be unproductive. The key is to understand which weaknesses are important enough to address.

Ask yourself the following question to determine if addressing a weakness is worth your attention:

Does the weakness get in the way of my top 1% performance?

Remember, the goal is to focus on the weaknesses that are essential to improve in order to perform at your highest level. If your goal is to run a company and inspire people to embrace your vision, you will need to improve your leadership capabilities if they are lacking. If your goal is to learn how to scuba dive and you can barely swim, you will have to learn to swim. However, if you have no desire to scuba dive, then it may not matter that swimming is a weakness. Similarly, you may not need to work on your "people" skills if you work with numbers instead of people during the day. On the other hand, if you have a customer service position you may need to focus on these skills. You need to be aware of what you are striving to achieve and what type of impact you can make if you address the weakness.

Once you decide which weaknesses are critical to your success and which ones are not worthy of your time, then decide how much time you should invest learning the skills you want to improve and what important details you will need. Keep reminding yourself that only *some* weaknesses need to be addressed and improved.

Remember, you do not need to be a hero in everything you do. Effective leaders and CEOs understand that the goal is not to be the best at everything, just to bring out their best in areas that matter and to know their weaknesses. The rest can be delegated to others with more appropriate skill sets. The practice of delegating will be discussed further in Ritual Six. Focus on investing effort where you will see the biggest impact to YOU INC. You *can* be a top 1%er without turning every weakness into a strength.

WEAKNESS MAKEOVER

Once you have determined which weaknesses are worth spending time to improve, use this four-step approach to start your weakness makeover. You can use the *IDEAS* page at the end of this ritual to jot down any thoughts as you work through this exercise. It is important to not only identify the weakness, but also to note the reason it needs to be addressed.

1. COMMIT TO THE WEAKNESS YOU WANT TO IMPROVE

Stop talking about all the changes you want to make. Commit to an area in the YOU INC. blueprint that, if improved, could make an immediate impact in your life. Too many people prefer complaining about what is wrong and make up excuses for why they can't do something. Either let something go or do something about it. Those are your two choices.

2. BELIEVE YOU CAN DO IT

Mindset is the name of the game. We all have weaknesses and are often frustrated by them. Note that improving an area that makes a difference in your life does not mean striving for perfection. Your focus should be on making progress. Instead of telling yourself "I'm a bad public speaker," say, "I can practice to become a better public speaker."

3. CHOOSE ONE STEP AND MOVE INTO ACTION

There are a host of small steps that could help you improve. List them all and then prioritize the steps that will yield the biggest result. Start with an easy step, and as your confidence builds, take on bigger challenges. Small steps *will* lead to big results. If one of your weaknesses is making the time to stay in touch with important people in your life, a few small steps could include making a list of ten people to connect with, spending ten minutes each day to call or send an email, and scheduling one dinner a week with a person on your list.

4. STAY ON COURSE

Realize that turning a weakness around will take effort and hard work. There will be many times you feel like quitting and turning back. Remind yourself why improving this weakness is important in the first place and then recommit to your actions. You can always refer back to your reasons on the *IDEAS* page.

TOP 1% TIP: Do not try to fix all of your weaknesses at once. Make a list of each thing that you would like to improve and start by choosing one weakness to focus on. Write down why this area is important to address and what changes you need to make for it to have a positive impact in your life. Outline three things that you can do to start the process. Then follow the steps in the Weakness Makeover above.

BOTTOM LINE SUMMARY

RITUAL THREE: EXCEL WITH YOUR STRENGTHS
Identify and use your key strengths

Living in your top 1% builds upon your core strengths to produce your personal best. Your ability to recognize and apply your strengths will restore confidence and keep you centered. It is much more effective to face challenges when you are standing on two feet rather than trying to balance on one foot. It will not make the challenges vanish, but it will give you a better chance to brave the changing elements. Make it a ritual to use the strengths that let you be authentic and bring out your best. Keep in mind you only need to address the weaknesses that matter.

KEY PRACTICES TO HELP YOU EMBRACE THIS RITUAL

1. Identify and use your strengths to lead you into an upward spiral.

2. Apply your strengths in both routine and challenging situations for best results.

3. Focus on improving only those weaknesses that, if improved, can add value and enhance YOU INC.

TOP 1% PEP TALK

You've assessed YOU INC., your mindset, and your strengths and weaknesses. You are at a fork in the road, and you need to make a choice. Will you stay on the same road or switch your route? I hope you have experienced some thoughts that have opened your eyes and heart to what is possible. Now turn the page and set your wheels into motion by designing some meaningful goals in Part II of the book.

IDEAS

PART 2: CREATE

We ask ourselves, 'Who am I to be brilliant, gorgeous, talented, and fabulous?' Actually, who are you not to be?

MARIANNE WILLIAMSON

RITUAL FOUR

GO FOR THE GOAL

It's not what you start in life, it's what you finish.

KATHARINE HEPBURN

In 1961, in a speech before congress, President John F. Kennedy announced that he wanted to send a man to the moon. He declared, "I believe that this nation should commit itself to achieving this goal, before the decade is out, of landing a man on the moon and returning him safely to earth." Even NASA did not know what approach it would use to achieve this feat. Many people were skeptical about sending a man to the moon. On July 20, 1969, this goal was accomplished.

Top 1%ers set specific and measurable goals that provide a sense of purpose and heighten overall self-esteem and satisfaction in their lives. If the word "goal" is too daunting, then substitute a more appealing word, such as *purpose, aim, desire,* or any other word that resonates with you. A more approachable way to think about goals is to view them as a path that will increase your chances of a desired outcome.

What would you love to accomplish that would bring you great joy and fulfillment? Do you want to complete your college degree? Would you like to carve out time to take ballroom dancing classes? Perhaps it is time to start a new career that truly excites you such as a restaurant owner, a landscape architect, or a writer of children's books. Once you have decided on an outcome that is meaningful to you, you will be able to decide which goals to pursue.

There are three core phases to the goal setting process: *The Why*, *The How*, and *The What Now*. To be effective with your goals you will need to work through each phase and follow through. Setting a goal and not taking the next step is equivalent to organizing your birthday party and then not showing up. You have to show up for your goals, roll up your sleeves, and get involved. As you move through the goal setting process consider what you can do differently this year than in previous years to achieve your top 1%.

PHASE I: THE WHY

You may ask, "Why do I need to set goals and challenge myself?" There are various links between the benefits of setting goals and leading a happy, productive, and rewarding life. Setting goals gives you a powerful starting point and foundation on which to develop your talents. Extensive studies have been done on the positive impact of setting goals. Sonja Lyubomirsky, in her book *The How of Happiness*, offers compelling research to support this theme. "People who strive for something personally significant, whether it's learning a new craft or changing a career, are far happier than those who do not have strong dreams or aspirations. Find a happy person, and you will find a project." People who lack meaningful goals have lower productivity levels. To live in your top 1%, you will need to set goals that drive you closer to a desirable outcome.

Goals are an effective way to make sure you do not leave any of your potential on the table. Even a small amount of progress can be the momentum you need to make a change. Chances are, you will be further along than if you did nothing. Regardless of the outcome, you will learn something from the experience. Once you open your eyes to what you can achieve, you will be able to see the world of possibilities that exists.

BENEFITS OF SETTING GOALS

Anyone who has worked toward a goal and enjoyed moments of great satisfaction can attest to the benefits below, regardless of the outcome. It is likely that you have experienced many of these benefits during your own goal setting process. Goals help to:

- Create the vision for where you want to go.
- Clarify priorities.
- Enhance your motivation level.
- Provide a greater sense of excitement each day.
- Build confidence (the feeling of "I did it").
- Help you stay focused.
- Give you hope.
- Increase accountability and results.

The next time you decide to start a new business, improve your golf game, or focus on an important relationship in your life, think about what makes the goal meaningful and specific to you. Every goal has the potential to be great as long as it is one that you value and make a priority. The challenge is to design your goal so it empowers you to take action, yet does not overwhelm you.

The story below illustrates the power of goals and how they can make a positive difference in one's life.

ARNOLD'S STORY: What do a bodybuilder, blockbuster action hero, author, businessman, and California governor have in common—the ability to pursue goals, think without boundaries, and create a clear vision. Meet Arnold Schwarzenegger, who has achieved all of the above and more.

Arnold grew up in Austria. He was eighteen when he entered and won his first bodybuilding competition. He was passionate about bodybuilding and went on to become Mr. Universe and then Mr. Olympia seven times. His goal was to be the greatest bodybuilder in the world, and he did it.

His next goal was to become a movie star. Arnold moved to the United States in 1968 at the age of 21. He comments, "I arrived here with empty pockets but full of dreams, full of determination, full of desire." He was focused and worked hard to build a financial base while he pursued his acting dream. He was a savvy businessman from an early age and started a bricklaying business with a bodybuilder friend in California. They used the profits to start a mail order business selling bodybuilding and fitness equipment. He invested the profits from these ventures into real estate and purchased his first apartment building for $10,000. He continued to increase his real estate holdings and was a millionaire by the time he was thirty years old.

In 1977, he published a biography and appeared in a documentary, *Pumping Iron*, which got him noticed on the screen. He used this recognition to expand his career into movies. His goal of wanting to be a movie star was met by many obstacles. Arnold recalls, "It was very difficult for me in the beginning. I was told by agents and casting people that my body was 'too weird,' that I had a funny accent, and that my name was too long. You name it, and they told me I had to change it. Basically, everywhere I turned, I was told that I had no chance." His big break on screen was *Conan the Barbarian*. He went on to star in multiple blockbuster films and subsequently, became one of the highest paid actors in Hollywood. Mission accomplished.

Perhaps the biggest goal Arnold Schwarzenegger achieved was becoming the Governor of California. With limited political experience, he was elected in a recall election in 2003 and then re-elected for a second term in 2006. Similar to Arnold, you may be told you can't do something and will likely meet obstacles on your path. Specific goals and a clear vision are what helped Arnold. They can make a difference for you too.

Arnold's story of achieving and accomplishing multiple goals can be yours. He did not have special privileges or resources growing up, just dreams and the willingness to take action. He was an avid goal setter and wrote his goals at the beginning of each year on index cards. Arnold did not limit his accomplishments to what other people thought he was capable of achieving and did not restrict himself to setting goals in just one area of his life. You can substitute "bodybuilder" and his other accomplishments for whatever is important to you and apply this example to all the areas of YOU INC.

TAKEAWAY: Setting goals helps you to see beyond limits and achieve things that other people may say are impossible.

PHASE II: THE HOW

Once you are convinced of the importance or *The Why* of setting goals, you will need to focus on *The How* to set a goal. The goal setting process is clear-cut once you get it right. It will be complicated if you get caught up in the maze of "Why did I set this goal?" As you begin to think about your own goals and what you want to pursue, it is essential that you put a system in place. You probably have many maps that are hard-wired into your mind that help you complete various tasks in your life. You most likely have a map for your morning routine at home, how you get to work, and what you do to start your workday. Do you have a map for your goal setting process? This is the time to create new maps and systems in your life to support your growth and learning.

The goal setting process is about focusing on what you want to achieve within a given time frame. Therefore, you want to reinforce what you can do in the different areas of your life. The following *checkpoints* will help you set effective goals:

☑ Add powerful words to write your goal such as "I will," "I am," and "I can."

☑ Avoid using negative or unconvincing words such as "can't," "try," "maybe," or "hopefully."

☑ Identify a positive outcome rather than a negative one such as "I will arrive at my appointments with time to spare so I can relax" vs. "I won't be late," or "I will maintain my ideal healthy weight" instead of "I will not eat bread."

THE GOAL SETTING PROCESS: STRATEGIES FOR SUCCESS

What sets top 1%ers apart from people who settle for something less than their best is the ability to set goals and then take action. It's simple to set a goal and not follow through. The real challenge is to design a meaningful goal and make it happen.

Anyone can set a goal. There is no official goal czar that approves your goal and determines whether your goal is exciting, meaningful, or important to pursue. Top 1%ers start with a compelling vision that pulls them closer to their goal. They design goals that the goal czar would approve if he did indeed exist.

A common approach to setting goals is to use the acronym SMART. This helps people to focus on setting goals that are Specific, Measurable, Attainable, Realistic, and Timely. Although SMART goals can be an effective starting place, you will need to do more to reach your top 1%. The following seven strategies will help to make your goals come alive:

1. START WITH THE IDEAL SITUATION

Top 1%ers start with the ideal scenario, and then work backwards. What would you love to achieve by the end of the year? Pretend for a moment that you are having dinner and sharing all the wonderful things that happened in the last year. What would you want to share with your friends, family, and co-workers? Think about things that would bring you great pleasure and you would be proud to share.

Is it time to take your yoga practice to the next level and become a certified yoga instructor? Does it interest you to take a cooking class and finally have that dinner party you've been talking about? Or, would it add meaning to your life to spend more time with your nieces and nephews and really be involved in their life? Push yourself to set the obstacles aside and focus on what you would love to see happen in your life. Dream a little and then focus on the goals that genuinely excite you.

Refer back to the YOU INC. blueprint and think about what you would like to change or improve in each area. Think about what would make you happy in order to bring more pleasure into your life. It will be helpful to write down your thoughts on the *IDEAS* page.

2. GO FOR GOALS THAT ARE IMPORTANT AND EXCITING TO YOU

Top 1%ers strive for goals that are intrinsic and authentically meaningful. They become a doctor or a fireman because they want to help people rather than satisfy their family. Choose goals that are exciting to *you* rather than others. Take a moment and think about *why* each goal is important to you. What will the impact be if you achieve this goal? If you are not excited to reach a specific outcome, then do not spend your precious time and energy achieving it. While some people may want to be the top salesperson in a company, that goal may not appeal to you.

Often reaching a goal will require that you make sacrifices in your life, such as giving up personal time or losing sleep. Top 1%ers know what is important to them and understand they will have to prioritize so they can make the necessary adjustments to reach their goals. You will undoubtedly face various obstacles along your path that will force you to make difficult decisions, so the more passionate you are about your goals, the greater success you will have in moving past these challenges.

3. ALIGN GOALS AND VALUES

Top 1%ers successfully align goals with their core values. Values are the core ingredients for how to live your life: what you care about, what fuels your decisions, and what propels you to make the extra effort. Values help you stay focused and create sustainable change because you tap into what truly matters. When you weave values into your goals, you experience a greater sense of purpose, therefore finding it easier to stay on track. If you want to lose fifteen pounds but health is not a core value, you will find it challenging to stay motivated. A client's top value was to be adventurous. I helped him realize that travel energized him and made him happy. As a result, he regularly set up fun weekend trips with friends.

If you need help identifying your values, think of the two role models you selected in the beginning of the book. What values do they use to guide their actions? It may be helpful to think of a character in a book you like, or traits of people in your life that you respect. Examples of values include adventure, compassion, creativity, faith, family, friendship, generosity, health, honesty, humor, knowledge, love, passion, and respect.

4. USE THE POWER OF THE PEN

Top 1%ers put their words on paper. Many people talk about their goals, yet few people actually write them down. It makes a difference. You need to see and feel your goal to perform at your highest potential. When you write down your goals, it makes you personally accountable. It is one of the most sacred steps you can take because you enter into a contract with yourself. Writing your goals helps you close the gap between where you are and where you want to go.

There are many ways to write down your goals. Some people prefer to use a journal or inspiration book for their ideas and others write their goals on a note card that they can easily take with them, or post them on a mirror in their house. One of my rituals is to write down my goals at the beginning of each year on an oversized piece of paper, and then transfer them to my computer in the top 1% goals folder. I also import them to my Blackberry so I always have them handy. I continue to fine-tune them during the year and add new goals as well.

TOP 1% TIP: Take five minutes and decide where to write your goals. Some useful ideas include keeping a goal sheet in your wallet, using your goal as a login for your computer, or posting your goals as a screen saver. Perhaps you want to buy a special notebook that has a meaningful and inspiring cover. You can also write down quotes that inspire you or tape pictures to the pages that lift your spirits. There are many ways to remind yourself in writing of what you really want. Think about what will work most effectively for YOU INC.

5. CRAFT CLEAR-CUT GOALS

Top 1%ers set clearly defined goals. If I told you I wanted to be a better cook or be a better tennis player, would you know what I meant? How would these goals be measured to see if I made any progress? Often, clients set vague goals without even realizing they are vague. Any goal with the words *more*, *better*, or *try* needs to be fine-tuned so that it is clear what you plan to achieve. If you want to eat better or get in better shape, does that mean you want to feel energized during the day, be a vegetarian, lose ten pounds, fit into your jeans from college, run a marathon, or be able to keep up with your young children?

I went to a conference in Los Angeles and I sat next to a man who told me his goal was to build his business. This is a classic example of a vague goal. How could he track his success without having a measurable goal or progress markers? "Growing your business" could mean getting ten new clients in the next three months, opening a second office within six months, or increasing revenues by 30% by the end of the year. If you leave it to chance, you have to hope for the best instead of create your best. The more specific you can be with your goal, the better the result. This means stating specifically what you will do and including a timeframe. Consider the following examples before you start writing your goals:

VAGUE GOAL: I hope to build my business this year.

☑ *CLEAR-CUT GOAL:* I will increase revenues by at least 15% by the end of this year.

VAGUE GOAL: I will try to reduce my debt and start managing my finances better.

☑ *CLEAR-CUT GOAL:* I will make a weekly budget and pay down $200 of my debt each month.

VAGUE GOAL: I want to be a good parent.

☑ *CLEAR-CUT GOAL:* I will make time to read to my children at least three nights per week for twenty minutes.

VAGUE GOAL: I want to exercise more this year.

☑ *CLEAR-CUT GOAL:* I will stretch and practice yoga three times per week to maintain a strong and healthy body.

TOP 1% TIP: *Read your goal out loud and ask yourself if it is absolutely clear what you are striving to achieve and why it is important. If your goal was posted as a road sign would it clearly direct you to a specific destination? Keep fine-tuning your goal until it feels right. Only you know what's best for YOU INC.*

---

6. MAKE YOUR GOALS HARMONIOUS

Top 1%ers design their goals to complement one another. If you start a new business, which requires weekly travel to visit clients and simultaneously want to spend quality time with your family, you need to realize that these goals will compete against each other. If you are traveling, it will be difficult to have dinner with your family consistently. Both of these goals are important, but you will need to prioritize them depending on your values.

If you pursue too many goals at the same time that are non-harmonious, you will get frustrated when you do not achieve your desired results. This does not mean your goal is a bad goal, it just means that the timing may be off, or that you did not take the time to carefully think about how to prioritize them. As you write down your goals, make sure to cross-check them and decide what you need to do to make them harmonious. This means looking at the time, energy, and resources that each will require. Being realistic and honest with yourself from the beginning will help you to stay on track.

7. STRETCH YOURSELF

Top 1%ers reach a bit higher and set *stretch* goals. When you set a stretch goal you strive for something that you might not have thought possible. Just to clarify, it does not mean that you have to be No. 1 or the best in whatever you do. What would be fantastic to achieve by the end of this year? This is your moment to shine. Stretch yourself a little and let yourself dream. It takes just as much effort to aim high as it does to aim low. A stretch goal could be writing your first book and striving to be on the best-seller list, starting a foundation and raising $25,000 the first year, opening a design firm and having ten clients within six months, or running your first five kilometer race in under thirty minutes. Each person will have a different set of stretch goals.

One important note: it is ok if you do not reach your entire stretch goal by the date you targeted. Simply start from where you are and fine-tune your goal to include new milestones and a new completion date. Chances are you will be much further along than if you set a vague goal or did not set a goal at all.

SETTING YOUR GOALS

What goals are you going to set this year? What would you really love to achieve? By now you should have some ideas for the goals you would like to pursue in different areas of the YOU INC. blueprint. I encourage you to use the *IDEAS* page to start getting your thoughts on paper. Later you will be able to transfer them to the *GOALS WORKSHEET*. This is the moment of truth.

For every goal you set, ask yourself the following questions to make sure the goal is meaningful to you before you move forward:

- Why is the goal important?
- What impact will completing the goal have on your life?
- Are you ready to commit to the goal on good and challenging days?
- Where does the goal fall on your list of priorities?
- Do you believe you can accomplish this goal?

Two of my goals are to be a speaker at The Women's Conference in California in 2011 and to be in a meaningful relationship with someone who challenges and inspires me. My goals share two common themes: they are a priority, and they are meaningful to me. Here's an inside look at how I've outlined these two goals.

	CAREER (STRETCH GOAL)	RELATIONSHIPS
GOAL	I will be a speaker at the Women's Conference in 2011 and receive positive feedback from the audience.	I will be in a fabulous, loving, and energizing relationship.
IMPORTANCE	I want to inspire others to go after their goals and build a community of top 1%ers.	I want to share and experience life with someone I care about.
PRIORITY (EXPLAINED IN PHASE THREE BELOW)	Tier One.	Tier One.
SMALL STEPS (EXPLAINED IN PHASE THREE BELOW)	Look at the conference website for contact information.	Make a list of all the qualities that I want in a person, categorizing them by "must haves," "nice to haves," and include any "deal breakers."
	Send an email to learn more about the process of becoming a speaker.	Commit to meeting new people by attending at least one social function a week.
	Contact three former speakers to learn how they got connected.	Buy a book that offers helpful advice on how to be your best in relationships.
CHALLENGES	Past speakers are usually well-known or famous.	Find someone I am compatible with and who inspires me.
TARGET DATE (ALWAYS INCLUDE A DATE)	October 2011.	Ongoing, Summer 2011.

The goal setting process is often more difficult than it appears. You have to identify what you are going for and decide to make it a priority. It may take some time to fully develop a detailed goal. The next section helps you break down your goals into manageable parts and take action.

PHASE THREE: THE WHAT NOW

It takes a lot of courage to say you are going to do something and go for a goal that is personally meaningful. Will this be the year you accomplish your goals and feel a tremendous sense of satisfaction or will it be the year you say you are going to do something and then let the opportunity pass? You are at another fork in the road and you have to make a choice. What now? This phase is about prioritizing goals, taking small steps, and staying motivated on your path. Personal fulfillment comes from taking responsibility and being the CEO of your goal setting process.

PRIORITIZE YOUR GOALS

The goal setting process is tricky because many think the process is finished once they set their goal. On day one you feel empowered when you declare what you are going to do. Day two is when the story gets interesting. Will you be able to stay committed?

Once you have all your goals on paper, you need to prioritize them. Depending on the person, the goals will have different priority levels. Many people find it helpful to prioritize their goals by highlighting their *tier one* goals first. These are the goals that are most meaningful and have the greatest impact on YOU INC. They are not necessarily the goals that help you make the most money or bring a promotion but rather the goals that either satisfy your basic survival needs or add a greater sense of fulfillment.

Think about which goals require your attention right now. Although your end goal may be to take a one-week vacation in the next six months, you have to first consider your immediate needs. For example, you may need to pay your health insurance premium or the monthly payment for your student loan before you can spend any additional money. Be sure to consider your basic needs first.

Is it more important to find a new place to live, reduce your debt, adopt a dog, go back to school and get a degree, change jobs, focus on your relationship, buy a new car, or eat healthier and reduce your cholesterol? If you are in danger of having a heart attack, then reducing your cholesterol and losing weight would be a *tier one* goal. However, if changing your healthy living rituals can be reworked over the year, it may not have to be the top priority. Similarly, if you want to move forward in your career and need a degree, then this goal may become a *tier one* priority.

This is a challenging but important step in the process so take an extra moment to clarify what you want. Setting priorities will help you stay accountable and reduce your stress levels. This will help you lay out the best path to living in your top 1%.

Another success check is to evaluate what impact pursuing a goal in one area will have on another area of YOU INC. For example, if you want to change jobs and start a new exercise program, will you have the time and energy to juggle both of these goals at the same time? Although both are important, you may have to fine-tune each goal so that they are harmonious and aligned with your vision.

If you feel that all of your goals are top priorities, then you will need to allocate your time to what needs to be done first. An essential step is to break down each goal into smaller parts and then decide what you need to attack initially. This reality check is critical.

SMALL STEPS = BIG RESULTS

The secret of getting ahead is getting started. The secret of getting started is breaking your complex, overwhelming tasks into small, manageable tasks, and then starting on the first one.

MARK TWAIN

People who live in their top 1% understand that small steps are the key to building confidence and helping you adjust to the process of change. Goals must be broken down into small steps if you plan to follow through and make your objectives a reality. Small steps are synonymous with action and ignite the goal setting process. The Japanese refer to this idea as *kaizen*, or "continuous improvement." The secret is that both major and minor changes happen one step at a time. This is counterintuitive for many people who believe big steps are the only way forward. Some people approach challenges with an all or nothing mindset, such as not eating sugar for the month, working every day till 10 p.m., or going to the gym seven days a week at 5 a.m. This approach may work temporarily but it will not be sustainable over time.

The question to ask yourself is, "What is *sustainable* given my lifestyle?" How many priorities can you juggle without sacrificing your best at work, home, and for yourself? Research shows that when you take on more than you can handle, your goals get derailed.

For example, reading a four hundred page book, buying a home, and driving cross-country could all be overwhelming tasks, but when you break them down into small steps, these tasks become achievable. Consider the following small steps toward the following big accomplishments.

- If you read just twenty pages a day of a four-hundred-page book, you will finish the book in twenty days without much effort. Even if you miss a day, you can finish the book within the month.

- If you view three new homes once a week, you will see twelve homes a month and will begin to gain valuable market knowledge.

- If you drive four hundred miles a day, you can drive from New York City to Los Angeles, California, and enjoy sunshine and warmth in seven days!

Without small steps, you feel overwhelmed and do not know where to start. If you fall off-track or go a few days without taking a small step, simply start where you are and get back into action as soon as you can. Progress comes from focusing on what you *can* do rather than what you *did not* do. Big ideas become possible to achieve when you take that first small step.

> **TOP 1% TIP:** *Give yourself ten minutes right now and take care of one small thing that you have been talking about doing for a while. You could delete unnecessary files from your computer, organize one small area in your house, or clean out the trunk of your car. You will be amazed how much you can accomplish in ten minutes.*

PAM'S STORY: Pam Koner, a 2009 CNN HERO, set her crusade in motion with one phone call. Her call to action started when she saw a photograph in *The New York Times* of an eight-year-old girl in Pembroke, Illinois who was in need of food. The 57-year-old single mom with two children called an outreach worker in Pembroke who confirmed that the town desperately needed food. Pam recruited families in her neighborhood to join the cause and donate food and household essentials. She eventually created *Family-to-Family*, a nonprofit organization that connects families who want to make monthly food donations to families in need. The organization has donated 800,000 meals to families in thirteen communities.

Pam did not have any special resources or connections. She cared and was motivated to take action. Her goal was to make a difference and improve the lives of others. Her one small step of making a phone call has made a significant impact in Pembroke and many other communities. Pam proved that anyone can be a hero.

> *TAKEAWAY: One small step can uncover potential where you did not even realize it existed.*

BENEFITS OF SMALL STEPS

The journey of a thousand miles begins with a single step.

LAO-TZU

Small steps have powerful applications to help you achieve your vision and goal. They help you to:

1. BREAK DOWN GOALS INTO MANAGEABLE PARTS

Small steps pave the road to success by making it easier to achieve your goal. If you want to get in shape or lose weight, your small steps could include joining a gym, buying running shoes, calling a friend to walk together, or reading a book to learn about nutrition. If you want to change jobs, your small steps might be revamping your resume, connecting with several headhunters, looking online for job openings, and networking with friends. One step will not complete the process but it can be a powerful launch pad. The key is to continuously identify the small steps you can take to achieve your goal. Train yourself to write down as many small steps as you can to track your progress. You will feel empowered by each small step you get to check off as "completed" and be able to see and feel yourself getting closer to your goal.

2. BUILD CONFIDENCE

Small steps boost your confidence by allowing you to experience a series of small wins. This makes it easier for you to see how bigger steps and projects are possible. Often, people focus on what went wrong during the week instead of what went well. Highlighting weekly wins is a great practice to implement into your rituals. A weekly win simply identifies something that went well during the week or a positive step you took toward your goal. It's a great way to start your day or a meeting and makes you feel good about yourself. For example, a weekly win could include spending quality time with your children, taking a spin class at the gym, or having a productive call with a client.

3. REDUCE THE FEELING OF BEING "STUCK"

Whether you have a big or small vision, if you feel stuck, you are not making forward progress. As soon as you feel stuck, think of a small step you can take to move forward. Refocus your energy on this one small step, instead of stressing out over the final outcome, and it will put you back on the right path. For instance, if you are trying to find a job and have submitted over fifty resumes without any responses, you may feel "stuck." Try changing your approach by reaching out to former colleagues or classmates for a networking lunch. You could also set up an informational interview with a company you would love to work for.

4. LEAD YOU INTO AN UPWARD SPIRAL

As you build confidence in one area of your life, that feeling overflows into other areas and leaves you wanting to take on additional challenges. Smaller accomplishments can often elicit the same feeling as larger ones. They help you gain an immediate boost both to your confidence levels and to what you believe is possible. This is a powerful yet simple concept that can make a significant difference in your life.

TOP 1% TIP: Share your goal and small steps with a friend who has experienced wins in the area you want to make progress. Their insights may or may not work for you but the more information you can gather, the better off you will be. You will feel empowered by declaring your small steps.

PETER'S STORY: Small steps lead to big results.

GOAL: My client, Peter, wanted to save $5,000 in twelve months.

IMPORTANCE: He wanted to build financial stability to increase confidence, have extra money to enjoy a vacation, and build a future with his partner.

CHALLENGES: Peter had $3,000 in credit card debt and did not save any portion of his paycheck because he enjoyed spending money.

SMALL STEPS:

- Shifted his mindset to start saving today.
- Tracked his weekly spending habits on a spreadsheet.
- Made a monthly budget and posted it on the refrigerator.
- Opened a savings account.
- Brought lunch to work instead of eating out during the week.

As a result, Peter paid off his credit card debt *and* increased his savings to $5,000 in less than nine months—the most he had ever saved. The savings resulted from taking small steps.

TAKEAWAY: Quantum leaps occur by breaking down your big ideas into small steps.

Whether your goal is to strengthen relationships at work, start a new hobby, save your marriage, or get promoted by the end of the year, there are effective small steps to take that will bring you closer to your goal. Jeff, a thirty-eight-year-old account manager at an advertising company, wanted to spend quality time with his family, so he started a log to track how many times a month he had dinner at home. It sounds trivial, but he had so many client dinners to attend that this simple step was the only way he could stay accountable. As a result, Jeff started having dinner at home four nights per week instead of two.

MY STORY: In 2007, I had set a goal to complete my first triathlon, the New York City Triathlon. There was one major problem—you have to swim, bike, and run to cross the finish line, and I had not been in a swimming pool in thirty years.

The race consisted of a 0.9-mile swim, 24.8-mile bike ride, and 6.2-mile run. I started my swim journey and took a tiny first step—I swam for six minutes, my max at the time. I could not swim one length of the pool without being completely out of breath. I needed some training. I took four swimming lessons to learn the basics and attended group swim classes at the gym to practice. As an athlete, I knew I could do better than six minutes, so I added a few minutes each time I went swimming. Four weeks later, I was swimming two times per week for twenty minutes. After three months I was ready to swim in the Hudson River. Finishing the swim, complete with jellyfish, was one of the most exciting accomplishments of my life because it was so far outside my comfort zone. This was only possible because I approached my goal with realistic small steps.

As a result of this win, I had the confidence to train for and complete my first half Ironman competition three years later (1.2-mile swim, 56-mile bike ride, and 13.1-mile run). When I doubt myself in the face of a new challenge, I remind myself of this special win and what is possible when you take small steps. Every top 1%er must master the small step approach.

TAKEAWAY: *Small steps = big results*

TAKING THE RIGHT SMALL STEP

Once a vision and goal are created, the hardest part is taking the right small step. We all like to accomplish a lot, so when we are losing weight, learning a new skill, or changing jobs, we often bite off more than we can chew. This approach will send your body into a fight-or-flight mode and your mission could be thwarted. You may want to reconsider if you are using an all or nothing approach. Choose your first step wisely because if it's not easily achievable, it could significantly derail your best efforts. First steps should help you build confidence and make you feel like you are a little closer to your goal.

How do you know if your *first* small step is the right one? The small step you commit to should feel doable and leave you feeling energized and willing to take on a follow-up challenge. Taking any small step that is *outside* your comfort zone will be a challenge. The right small step will minimize the shock and fear factor.

Top 1%ers keep it simple and start with what they know they can do, rather than think about all the obstacles on their path. They stay in the present moment and do not let future burdens derail or overwhelm them. Ask yourself three basic questions to determine if the small step is the right one:

1. IS THIS STEP TRULY REALISTIC?

You will have a gut feeling. If you want to be a first-time dog owner, does it make sense to adopt three dogs at once? It is probably best to start with one dog and then add to the family.

2. HOW CONFIDENT ARE YOU IN COMPLETING THIS STEP ON A SCALE OF 1 TO 10?

If you are a 7 or lower, you need to come up with a small step that you are confident you can complete.

3. WHEN WILL YOU COMPLETE THE STEP?

If you do not want to set a date and be accountable, that may be telling you the small step (or maybe even the goal) is not the right one.

Although one small step will make a big difference, the power is in taking multiple small steps to see progress. Many clients enjoy making it a ritual to reward themselves as they get closer to their ultimate goal. The reward can be getting yourself a subscription to your favorite magazine or splurging and treating yourself to a massage. The examples below highlight a few possible small steps that would be helpful.

FUN & CREATIVITY GOAL

I will adopt a dog by the end of the year.

Small Steps

Check with the landlord to see if you can have a dog in your building.

Talk to dog walkers and friends to make sure you will be able to take care of the new addition to your family.

Research the personalities of different breeds to determine what type of dog you want to adopt.

Visit a shelter for a potential dog to add to your family.

Many steps later...find the one!

HEALTHY LIVING GOAL

I will complete my first 10K race this summer.

Small Steps

Search online for potential races in your area.

Register for a race.

Join a running group.

Start with a short twenty-minute run, and then build your mileage over the next eight weeks.

Many steps later...finish your race!

Before you move on to the next ritual, I encourage you to take as much time as you need to write down your goals and small steps using the *GOALS WORKSHEET* at the end of the book to guide you through the process.

MOTIVATION CHECKPOINTS

Successful people create wealth as a byproduct of their passion and creativity.

MIKE MILKEN

Motivation is tied to commitment. You need to be motivated on the day you set your goal, when you take action, and when obstacles arise. It helps if you are optimistic and believe things will work out for you. When you have a setback, you can view it as a failure and feel helpless to change it, or view it as a *temporary* setback and still believe you can succeed.

Martin Seligman, a thought leader in positive psychology, did a study on optimism with insurance salespeople from MetLife. Seligman found that optimistic salespeople sold thirty-seven percent more than pessimistic salespeople in their first two years at MetLife. One explanation was that successful salespeople are used to hearing rejections and do not view them as failures. Optimistic people take setbacks in stride and see a way forward. They stay hopeful, do not take feedback personally, and realize that some days will be better than others. *Failure is a starting point rather than an end point.*

Motivation levels go up and down for everyone. Something that seems like an exciting idea at the beginning of the year may not hold your attention as other priorities arise. Unexpected events will happen that could easily throw you off course. These motivation checkpoints will help you stay on track:

- ☑ Expect obstacles along the way and ask yourself, "How important is it to reach my goal?"

- ☑ Double check that you are 100% committed to achieving your goal (meaning even when you are tired, busy, and do not feel like it).

- ☑ Take small steps and set milestones to make progress.

- ☑ Think of an inspiring story of someone who overcame challenges and what he or she did to stay motivated.

- ☑ Revise your goal to reflect any changes in your life.

Review these checkpoints whenever your motivation dips.

MARK'S STORY: Mark decided to travel and take time off from his career to pursue his passion for adventure and culture. His goal was to travel solo around the world and visit forty different countries. For two years, he worked two jobs and eighty hours a week to save enough money to travel. During the day he worked as a teacher and at night he bartended. He had to scale back his current lifestyle to save money and did not have as much time to spend with friends. He kept moving forward toward his goal by telling friends about his plans, bringing a map of the world to his bartending job, and hanging motivational phrases in his house. The most challenging part was taking the first step: finding a night job to start making extra money. Mark never lost sight of the importance of his dream as he diligently took all the small steps he needed to get there. He achieved his goal, traveled to various countries including Iraq, Bosnia, Vietnam, and Turkey, and learned to communicate in fifteen different languages.

Mark experienced incredible personal growth because he stayed motivated while he pushed himself outside his comfort zone. He gained confidence each step of the way and, at the end of this journey, he felt like he could take on any challenge.

> TAKEAWAY: *You may have to make sacrifices along the way, but when you combine small steps with the internal drive to achieve your goals, you become unstoppable.*

Whether your goal is to travel around the world, climb Mount Everest, or change careers, it starts with an idea and takes shape because of your motivation. Jordan Romero saw a mural at his school when he was nine years old and decided he wanted to climb Mount Everest. He and his parents made the dangerous trek, although many thought he was too young. He had to persevere through high altitude, severe winds, and extreme temperatures (fifty degrees below zero) to complete his goal. It took fifty-one days to make it to the summit, and because of his commitment and determination, he completed his goal and became the youngest person to reach the summit. When your goal is important and is a priority, you will take small steps to make it happen.

BOTTOM LINE SUMMARY

RITUAL FOUR: GO FOR THE GOAL
Set goals annually and take one small step a day

If you have a dream, you will need a clear-cut goal and small steps to make it come true. Companies and individuals use goals and small steps to create something of value. The *San Francisco Chronicle* reported that the best-selling author John Grisham set a goal to write one page a day when he first started writing. I started this book with the small step of writing one hour each day.

In 1972, Nike started with the small step of creating one pair of shoes. The company introduced its running shoe called the Moon Shoe and gave the shoes to athletes competing at the U.S. Olympic Trials in 1972 to test. Thirty-eight years later, Nike is one of the most recognized global brands and has a shoe for almost every sport. Each small step adds up.

Top 1%ers use small steps as a powerful method to move forward and accomplish larger goals. A small step can be anything that helps you make progress. Sometimes it will take a lot of effort, and other times it will take consistency. I promise you are better off taking a small step than doing nothing!

KEY PRACTICES TO HELP YOU EMBRACE THIS RITUAL

1. Write down your goals and repeat them to yourself so you are crystal clear on your destination.

2. Pursue goals that are both important and a priority to you.

3. Take one small step toward your goal to build momentum and follow that up with a series of small steps to unleash your potential.

TOP 1% PEP TALK

You have done the heavy lifting. Now it's time to move past your obstacles and see what your potential looks like. You are closer than you think, so let's keep moving!

IDEAS

RITUAL FIVE

THINK WITHOUT OBSTACLES

No matter what happens, it is within my power to turn it to my advantage.

EPICTETUS

Thinking without obstacles is about creating a world filled with possibilities. This approach helps you think with a *can-do* mindset and lifts you into an upward spiral. It is about training your mind to focus on what you can achieve before you manage the obstacles on your path. As you adopt this way of life you will naturally focus on solutions and what you want to create, rather than why something *can't* be done. Top 1%ers understand that executing a great idea takes vision, effort, and the ability to overcome challenges. It is a skill and takes practice.

Dara Torres exemplifies the idea of thinking without obstacles. At age forty-one, she decided to explore her potential as an elite athlete and earned a spot on the United States Olympic Swim Team. Most people would not dream of competing in the Olympics after taking seven years off from training, but Dara had a different vision for herself. She set aside her obstacles such as age, five knee surgeries, and the physical changes that come with having a child, and prepared to compete in her fifth Olympics against athletes half her age. She trained in the pool five days a week for two hours and then in the gym four days a week for an hour and a half. She dreamed big and inspired millions of people to go after what they want.

Dara won three silver medals at the 2008 Beijing Olympics and proved her words that "the water doesn't know your age… [goals] may become harder to achieve, but your dreams can't stop because you've hit a certain age or you've had a child." She swam her fastest race ever in the 50-meter freestyle and set a new American record. Although she missed a gold medal by 0.01 seconds, her silver medal represented a top 1% moment because she showed what is possible when you move past obstacles. Her medal symbolized a personal best. This remarkable feat paved the way for her to enjoy other opportunities such as a book deal, speaking engagements, and media appearances. Dara looked beyond obstacles and so can you.

MY STORY: I was nervous to leave my finance career even though I knew I was not passionate about it. I had so many doubts. What would my family think? Would I be able to start over in my late thirties? Would I be able to make money in a new career?

I decided to focus on the life I wanted to create rather than what I was giving up. I thought about my life, and more specifically, how I wanted to spend my ideal day—helping others, writing, coaching, speaking, and having time to enjoy an outdoor, active lifestyle. Many people think that changing careers is not an option. I think the *only* option is to find a way to do what you enjoy.

Once I developed a vision, I enrolled in a Life and Executive Coaching program. I talked to my family and shared my ideas for a path outside of finance. They were cautious but supportive. Other people do not necessarily have to believe in your vision to validate your decision. Be prepared for both positive and negative feedback on your path. Many people will not be able to see your vision, but you cannot let their thoughts discourage you.

To pursue the life I wanted, I left my last finance job and moved to California, which I had been talking about for years. Thinking without obstacles helped me dream, move through my fear, and create a powerful vision. I continue to implement my plan and enjoy greater fulfillment and happiness in my career and life. Reaching your potential is a process that can be learned.

TAKEAWAY: *Top 1%ers see possibilities where others see obstacles.*

Is it possible to think completely without obstacles? Yes! Brian Scudamore, the founder of 1-800-GOT-JUNK, a multimillion-dollar business which collects and hauls away unwanted goods, set a lofty goal to expand his company into the thirty U.S. and Canadian cities larger than Vancouver. "I imagined pure potential, no limits and no obstacles," he says. "And we hit our goal 16 days early." There are no prerequisites to dreaming big. All you need is a focused mind.

Do other people have to see or agree with your vision? No! Ted Turner, a media mogul, took his vision for cable television and changed the news and cable world forever. In 1980, he launched Cable News Network, CNN, which provided the first twenty-four hour, all news television coverage on a global scale. Turner saw the untapped potential of cable television and understood that technology was changing. "All my life people have said that I wasn't going to make it. They laughed at me when I started CNN. They laughed at me when I bought the Braves. They laughed at me when I bought the Hawks. They laughed at me when I bought MGM." The other networks did not share his vision. In 1991, *Time* magazine named Ted Turner Man of the Year. He is largely responsible for bringing cable TV into the mainstream culture. CNN began with 1.7 million cable subscribers. In 2010, CNN was available in over 100 million U.S. households and 200 countries around the world.

Perhaps making a major change or pursuing your vision feels impossible to you right now. You may have a family to support, a mortgage, or a job that would be difficult to leave. Regardless of how major you believe these issues to be, they are simply speed bumps. No matter what your situation is, you can always take a small step toward living your ideal vision—it does not have to be all or nothing. The first step is dreaming about a future that excites you. If you give yourself the freedom to dream, a world with possibilities will open up.

OBSTACLES AND PROGRESS GO TOGETHER

Life begins at the end of your comfort zone.

NEALE DONALD WALSCH

Whichever road you choose to live in your top 1%, it is important to know that obstacles will show up. Do you think Google, Amazon, or Starbucks built their successful companies without facing any obstacles? All people who have achieved greatness have encountered obstacles on their path to creating something special. Consider the following achievers and the obstacles they overcame.

- Thomas Edison tried over two thousand experiments before he invented the light bulb.

- Frank Gehry's second-year architecture teacher told him he should try a different profession. Today, he is regarded as one of the world's greatest architects.

- Beethoven composed some of his greatest symphonies after he was deaf.

- J.K. Rowling, a best-selling author, told Oprah in an interview that the Harry Potter series almost did not happen. Twelve publishers rejected Rowling and her agent told her, "You will never make money selling children's books." She has sold more than 400 million books and the Harry Potter series is one of the most successful to date.

- Tony Hsieh, CEO of the online retailer Zappos, was told he could not sell shoes online or build a brand around customer service. He did just that with Zappos and sold the company to Amazon for $1.2 billion in 2009. He continues to run the company and serves as the CEO.

Obstacles and progress are necessary partners. You can't have one without the other. If it's snowing and you need to go grocery shopping, you can choose to do nothing and stay home. The snow is an obstacle, but getting to the store is not urgent or extremely important. If it's snowing and your child needs medicine from the pharmacy, you will drive to the store. Your child's health is more important than the obstacle, so you drive to the store. In this case, you are 100% committed to your child's health. The truth is, to make any goal or dream a reality, it will take perseverance and the ability to overcome challenges on your path. Either way, your goal will need to be a high priority.

The key step is to train your mind to create your ideal picture first. There is no benefit to focusing on obstacles before you know what you want to create. It will only limit your vision. The only thing stopping you from creating your ideal picture or outcome is you. Obstacles often help us be better, improve a plan, think creatively, and reach down into our tool kit and persevere.

> *TOP 1% TIP: Start a collection of your favorite inspirational quotes that keep you positive and motivated. Post them on your computer, refrigerator, or car dashboard so that you can read them whenever you need a mental boost. A few profound words can give you a new perspective when facing obstacles.*

CLASSIFY YOUR OBSTACLES

Obstacles are any thing, person, situation, or thought that hinders your progress. If it gets in your way or slows you down, it is an obstacle. Top 1%ers classify their obstacles rather than group them all together. This classification step is an important differentiator for living in your top 1% to avoid getting overwhelmed. Often we are conditioned to think that obstacles represent a "Do Not Enter" or "Road Closed Ahead" sign. In reality, you decide how the obstacle is defined and what the sign says.

Obstacles can be grouped into three categories:

1. SPEED BUMPS

These are obstacles that slow you down, but ultimately, you can get around them and stay on track with a clear and focused mind. These obstacles can range from an employee calling in sick, to being stuck in traffic, or losing your phone.

2. DETOURS

These obstacles often force you to be crafty and devise a Plan B or alternate solution. You still arrive at your destination, but it takes commitment and extra effort. These obstacles can range from arriving at your hotel on a holiday weekend to learn you do not have a reservation and the hotel is fully booked, to not getting hired by the firm of your choice, or having the buyer for your house withdraw his bid and the sale falling through.

3. ROADBLOCKS

These obstacles can derail you unless you are focused, determined, and committed to your goal and making progress.

These obstacles could include major events such as: having a health issue, getting fired, or losing a loved one.

Obstacles show up in all different forms: a person who battles cancer; a salesperson who loses his computer; and an event planner who organizes a huge fundraising event for a charity only to find out the keynote speaker is sick and cancels last minute. The point is, each person decides how he or she will classify and manage the obstacle. Each time you face an obstacle ask, "Am I still committed to achieving my goal?" or "What can I do to stay committed to my goal?" These questions will clarify the issue quickly.

> **TOP 1% TIP:** *As you create your roadmap, think about the road sign that best describes how you want to view obstacles. If you hit an unexpected detour you will not want to see a sign that says, "Dead End" or "No Outlet." Visualize what your sign looks like and what the words say to keep you on the right path. If helpful, draw a picture of your sign or create one on your computer and post it in a place where you can see it every day. Your sign could read, "Plan B One Mile Ahead" or "Regroup Next Exit."*

JEN'S STORY: This powerful story will change the way you view all obstacles. Some people were meant to change the world, and Jennifer Goodman Linn is one of them. Her energy and zest for life are contagious. I was fortunate enough to meet her in a spin class at the gym when I lived in New York City. She graduated from Duke and earned her MBA from Harvard. She had one major obstacle—she was diagnosed with cancer in 2004.

What does a top 1%er do when she finds out she has a major obstacle? She starts a charity with her husband called *Cycle for*

Survival and raises money for cancer research at Memorial Sloan-Kettering. It is an annual indoor cycling event with over twenty-five hundred cyclists riding to fight cancer. She convinced Equinox, a major gym, to be an official partner and recruited the best instructors to teach. On the Friday before the charity event in 2010, Jen found out she had cancer for the fifth time. That Sunday she rallied, inspiring thousands of people and raised $2.4 million. In just five years, this event has raised over $8.5 million. I'm honored to have organized teams that have raised over $50,000 for this charity. The event has already funded thirteen clinical trials that have resulted in new treatments for cancer patients.

Jen has never let cancer define her. She exemplifies the ability to persevere in challenging situations and to think without obstacles. In a *Wall Street Journal* article about giving back Jen said, "I might have cancer but cancer doesn't have me and the minute I change my life for the disease it wins." Obstacles will not stop you when your goal is compelling and you have a deep desire to succeed. Perhaps you will want to reconsider the next time you think your obstacle is insurmountable and are tempted to say, "I can't." Please note that obstacles do not play favorites. They surface regardless of your education, marital status, or how many dollars you have in the bank.

> TAKEAWAY: *You define how you view your obstacles. They do not define you.*

Top 1% CEOs, artists, managers, parents, musicians, and athletes are so skilled in working through obstacles that they view major obstacles as speed bumps or detours. Apolo Ohno, an eight-time speed-skating Olympic medalist, embraces the obstacles he faces in his training and journey. "As an athlete, I do not look back at the medals…I look at the struggles it took to get to this point. I can look at them and say, 'I got you.'" Your mindset and commitment level will determine how you view obstacles.

As your level of commitment increases, the obstacles related to that goal or situation decrease. This occurs because you are determined to do whatever it takes to achieve your goal and overcome any obstacles that may stand in your way. This relationship holds for business, relationships, personal growth, and more. Think about a time in your life when nothing could stop you on your path. Maybe you were determined to prove yourself to your first boss, get your driver's license, buy your first home, go on vacation, recover from an injury, or build your business. Because your commitment to achieve your goal was off the charts, you worked through the obstacles. Commitment is like a light switch; it is either on or off. Top 1%ers are committed to achieving their goals and overcoming the associated obstacles.

TRACY'S STORY: My client Tracy wanted to start a family, but she was not in a relationship or married at the time. She was a nurse in her late thirties, and her ability to have a baby was a concern. She had various obstacles that would have caused many to give up. How would she take care of her baby as a single mom? Could she afford child care? Could she balance a full-time job, a baby, and still have time for herself?

Tracy wanted to explore her potential as a mother. She researched options and decided to adopt a baby from China. She saved enough money to pay for the adoption process and built a support team, which included her mom, two sisters, some close friends, and a nanny. It took five years to adopt her beautiful baby, and it was worth every moment.

Tracy experienced incredible joy by focusing on what she *could* do given her circumstances. The most fulfilling part of her journey was giving her daughter a chance to thrive and reach her greatest potential in a supportive environment rather than in the orphanage. When you think beyond obstacles, you give yourself opportunities to reach your optimal potential.

> TAKEAWAY: *Every accomplishment worth pursuing is accompanied by obstacles. Top 1%ers make the most out of what they have.*

OBSTACLES CAN BE OVERCOME

If an obstacle prevents you from moving forward, it needs to be addressed. Obstacles are viewed as such because we do not control the "event." We can however, control our reaction. Obstacles are objective facts. If your car does not start and you need to get to work, that's a valid obstacle. A person who is committed will find a way to get to work, whereas a person with a lower commitment level may not. You can choose to find a solution to an obstacle or let it change your course.

Kristi Yamaguchi, Olympic gold medal winner in figure skating, was born clubfooted, had plaster casts on her legs, and wore corrective shoes until she was two. She had desire, worked hard, and practiced rituals to become a champion. She visualized her performance the day and night before her competitions. She told herself she had "trained and was ready."

She had real obstacles and overcame them. Sometimes the most difficult obstacle is your ability to shift your mindset. *You are not the only one that faces obstacles. We all have them. If others can move through them so can you.*

You do not have to be a successful athlete or business leader to view obstacles through the lens of "I can do this." Think twice before you categorize a speed bump as a show-stopping obstacle. Reflect back on the two people you selected at the beginning of the book. How do they manage the obstacles they face? Top 1%ers choose to think without obstacles and go after what they believe they can achieve.

EXCUSES ARE A DIME A DOZEN

Excuses are tempting to use. They are plentiful, easy to think of, and free. The truth is, people who make excuses are not committed to accomplishing the task at hand. If you are late, there's always the traffic excuse. When it's rush hour in New York City, you will not be able to go across town in ten minutes. People who are on time prepare for traffic. Excuses are used to justify why you can't do something, when in fact you can.

Age, knowledge, time, and financial situation are other excuses that are tempting to use. How many times have you heard someone say, "I'm too old," "I do not know how," or "I'm not smart enough"? If you count yourself out before you even start, there is no way you will succeed. These excuses relate to your mindset and what you think you can achieve. Top 1%ers may not always have the skill set or knowledge, but they do have the commitment and desire to stretch and learn.

REDEFINE YOUR OBSTACLES

What obstacles are standing in the way of you moving forward? Use these exercises to help you gain clarity on potential roadblocks. You can use the *IDEAS* section to write down your thoughts.

- List all of your obstacles for each *tier one goal* identified in Ritual Four.

- Classify each obstacle and ask yourself, "Is this obstacle major enough to prevent me from moving toward my goal?" Either cross the obstacle off your list or move forward to the questions below.

- Write down three possible solutions to manage each obstacle.

- Double check to make sure you still want to pursue each goal from Ritual Four—revise your goal sheet as needed.

- Commit to taking one small step that helps you move past your obstacle.

Some of your obstacles are known ahead of time and others will surface on your path. You can use this same approach to effectively handle any unanticipated challenges along the way. Top 1%ers master the process of dealing with all types of obstacles without letting them hinder their progress.

TOP 1% TIP: As soon as an obstacle surfaces, make it a habit to immediately match it with a potential solution. Train yourself to think about what options you do have rather than waste your time analyzing what went wrong. Start by practicing on a small scale. For instance, if your dinner date cancels on you, immediately find a way to make productive use of that time.

BOTTOM LINE SUMMARY

RITUAL FIVE: THINK WITHOUT OBSTACLES
Visualize the ideal outcome

There will be obstacles in every area of the YOU INC. blueprint. You have to decide how you will view these challenges as you come to each new fork in the road. The goal is to focus on solutions that help you stay productive and view obstacles as speed bumps or detours. The key is to initially think in terms of the ideal situation as if there were no obstacles and then to effectively manage any challenges on your path. When you commit to thinking without obstacles, you take an oath that you will not make excuses. You will be amazed at what you can accomplish.

KEY PRACTICES TO HELP YOU EMBRACE THIS RITUAL

1. Train your mind to start thinking without obstacles and picture the ideal outcome.

2. Leave the self-imposed limitations behind and focus on what you can do.

3. Redefine your obstacles as speed bumps.

TOP 1% PEP TALK
It's time to start rolling forward now that you are dreaming about what can be. The views are beautiful from the summit. Take one more step forward and challenge yourself to see what you can do!
Now is the time to put into practice what you have learned from the top 1%ers around you and move into your stretch zone. How is your story developing to support your greatest potential?

IDEAS

LIVE IN YOUR STRETCH ZONE

A boat is always safe in the harbor,
but that's not what boats were built for.
Shared by KATIE COURIC
Women's Conference 2009, Long Beach, CA

Kenneth Cole is filled with passion, entrepreneurial spirit, and a sense for design and fashion. He has built a designer empire that includes shoes, clothes, and accessories for men, women, and children. He is known for his cutting-edge advertising campaigns that take a stand on current issues such as homelessness, AIDS, and "Get Out the Vote." His guiding principles have been innovation, creativity, and a willingness to move outside his comfort zone. In 2009, his company generated more than $400 million in revenue. The company has even been included on the *Forbes* magazine annual list of the "Two Hundred Best Small Companies in America."

Kenneth Cole started his company in 1982 during a recession. He designed his first line of women's shoes and had them manufactured in Italy. He was low on capital and knew this line needed to be successful or a second line would be unlikely. He learned Italian in order to supervise production at the factory and to make sure the shoes were ready in time for Market Week in New York City. Cole did not have enough money to set up a showroom, so he rented a truck to get buyers to notice his line of shoes. He changed the name of his company to Kenneth Cole Productions since the city only issued permits to utility and production companies. He rented a forty-foot trailer and filmed the movie *The Birth of a Shoe Company*. All the buyers visited his trailer, and he sold forty thousand shoes in two and a half days. Kenneth Cole Productions was in business.

Cole had an idea to make shoes and use a creative marketing strategy to get him noticed at Market Week. Are you like Kenneth Cole in having a mindset to take on new challenges, or do you prefer staying in your comfort zone? Consider all the inventions that have forced us to move outside our comfort zone—the automobile, the airplane, e-mail, cell phones, and social media sites such as Facebook. You may favor some of these inventions more than others, but all of them changed the way we function on a daily basis. People resisted many of these at first but then adapted to the ideas that were most beneficial. Top 1%ers opt for growth and choose to see what they can achieve.

Today is not a dress rehearsal.
KENNETH COLE

THE THREE ZONES OF ACTION

The zones of action illustrate the three different levels in which you function. You will often find yourself operating in different zones at different times. The act of shifting from zone to zone is a dynamic process. Once you learn how to manage these shifts, you will decrease your stress level significantly. As you become more competent in this flow, you will be able to take on new tasks. The only way to experience growth is to move outside your comfort zone and into your *stretch zone*. You must learn to become comfortable moving between the three zones.

1. COMFORT ZONE

The comfort zone holds your existing habits. It is where you feel most comfortable. Your stress levels and challenges are low. Your mind is less stimulated than in the stretch zone.

2. STRETCH ZONE

The stretch zone is about learning and growth. You continuously challenge yourself, and stress levels are manageable as you step through each new situation. Your mind is clear, focused, and often full of great insights.

3. STRESS/DANGER ZONE

The stress/danger zone leaves you feeling overwhelmed too much of the time. There is never any breathing space and you are stressed all the time. Your mind is cluttered, unfocused, and moments of clarity are rare.

The ideal zone to function in is your *stretch zone*. This is the zone where you are taking on new challenges, adapting, and building confidence. The challenge is to maintain living in the stretch zone without tipping over into the stress/danger zone. Often, people are not even aware of which zone they operate in. It will become easier to move into your stretch zone with practice. In which zone do you currently spend most of your time?

> **TOP 1% TIP:** *Challenge yourself and do one small thing that pushes you outside your comfort zone within the next week. Take a new class at the gym, go see a movie by yourself, try a different dish at your favorite restaurant, or make a cold call for your business. These little steps will help you get used to operating in your stretch zone.*

JESSICA'S STORY: Jessica Grant and I met in college and became friends. We shared many fun times in school but never realized just how soon she would achieve something special. After attending law school, Jessica worked as a defense attorney representing Fortune 500 companies in a variety of complex business matters. In her early thirties, she wanted to try something different, and switched sides to work at a smaller law firm to represent "the little guy." In her first case as a plaintiff's attorney, Jessica faced one of the largest, most profitable companies in the world, Wal-Mart. At the age of thirty-three, she became the lead counsel in what is now a landmark employment case, *Savaglio v. Wal-Mart*. It was the first wage-and-hour class action in the United States to go to trial against Wal-Mart, so the stakes were high.

For much of the litigation, Jessica went up against a Wal-Mart defense team comprised of several top-notch law firms and as many as twenty-three attorneys. Clearly out-muscled in terms of resources and staff, Jessica never let that intimidate her. She continually moved outside her comfort zone to learn about every facet of wage-and-hour law and always went the extra mile to keep pace with the experienced Wal-Mart team.

In 2005, after a four-month jury trial, Jessica obtained a $172 million jury verdict against Wal-Mart on behalf of the more than 116,000 California employees who were required to work all day without meal and rest breaks. The *National Law Journal* ranked this case as the largest verdict in an employment law case in 2005. Jessica received a *California Lawyer* Attorney of the Year Award and was named one of the "Top Women Litigators in California" by the *Daily Journal.*

When asked how she persevered over five years in the face of such overwhelming odds, Jessica said that although her journey often felt like scaling Mt. Everest, she stayed focused on taking small, manageable steps as opposed to thinking about the magnitude of what she was attempting to accomplish. Top 1%ers master the art of moving outside their comfort zone. The process becomes manageable with practice.

TAKEAWAY: Each day is an opportunity to redefine what's possible. When you move outside your comfort zone, you have the potential to produce extraordinary results that you may not have experienced otherwise.

MOVING OUTSIDE YOUR COMFORT ZONE

Many people feel good in their comfort zone. It is safe and you know what to expect. Safety is important when you are driving, but when you want to experience greater satisfaction in certain areas of your life, you have to stir things up and move outside your safety or comfort zone. The reality is: there is always a step you can take to raise your game. Review these three areas to see if you need to leave your comfort zone behind.

1. **PROGRESS:** Have you achieved all the things that are important to you?

This is a great time to take a moment and assess how the year is progressing. One of the hardest things to do is to honestly assess your progress. Are you really okay staying where you are, or is it time to venture out and take on a challenge, learn something new, or change jobs?

If you can't remember the last time you accomplished something that excited you, it is time to pursue a new challenge.

2. **MEANINGFUL GOALS:** Are you currently pursuing a goal that excites you?

Some goals are easier to achieve than others. When you strive for something just beyond your reach that matters, you will naturally want to move outside your comfort zone. The best reason to move forward is because you are motivated by a goal that challenges you and adds meaning to your life. The goal can be big or small.

If you have not set a goal in the last year that excites you, it is definitely time to leave your comfort zone behind.

3. **SMALL STEPS = BIG RESULTS:** Are you taking consistent small steps to achieve the results you want?

It's likely that you have several goals you would like to pursue. Setting a goal is just the beginning of the process and can be a false comfort zone unless you take small steps to make progress. Be honest with yourself, look at your goals and see when was the last time you took a small step forward.

If it has been longer than thirty days, you are ready to move outside your comfort zone with another small step.

MOVING OUTSIDE YOUR COMFORT ZONE
SUCCESS STORY

SEAN'S STORY: Sean worked as a manager for a radio station and was frustrated in his current role because he was working a lot of hours and not enjoying himself. He liked his co-workers and was comfortable with his routine at work, but was scared to make a change. He was nervous to look for a new job because he had worked in radio for eight years and felt like it was too late to start something new. He was in his comfort zone, but not where he wanted to be in his career. Sean had thought about changing industries for the last two years but never did anything about it because he believed he had limited skills to offer outside of radio.

We spent five sessions together over a two month period to help him identify his strengths, clarify what he loved to do, and explore how he was best suited to share his talents. He soon realized that he could turn his passions of coaching kids and athletics into his career. He was thrilled with the new vision but concerned because none of the jobs he wanted to pursue paid enough money to support his family and lifestyle.

I encouraged him to talk with his wife to share his issues. They realized they would have to make changes to their spending habits if he wanted to pursue a fulfilling but lower-paying job. Sean and his wife carefully analyzed the budget and looked for ways to creatively trim their expenses. They decided to eat at home instead of going out for dinner several times a week and asked their parents to watch the children on occasion instead of hiring a babysitter. They redesigned their budget to pave the way for Sean to start a career that he was excited about.

Sean became a personal trainer and high school basketball coach. During the summers, his plan was to start a day camp for kids. Two years later, he was making just as much money as he was in his previous job and loving his work. He had more time to spend with his children and be a dad. Sean was able to create his roadmap to living in his top 1% by pursuing a career he was passionate about and making changes to his life. The moment he was honest with himself, a new path became clear.

While it is inviting to stay in your comfort zone, progress happens when you take on a new challenge and have something to work toward. If you set a goal that motivates you and back it up with small and manageable steps, you will build confidence each step of the way. The challenge is to spend the majority of your time in the zone that helps you be your best.

> TAKEAWAY: Moving outside your comfort zone is a challenging process. Top 1%ers stick with that process to create new possibilities.

STRETCH INSTEAD OF STRESS

If you are in your stress zone all the time, you have to ask yourself what role you have in creating this atmosphere for yourself. Perhaps you are a busy CEO, or a parent with three children and no help. Both are valid reasons to be stressed, but there are plenty of CEOs and parents who are not stressed all the time.

You can experience stress both from positive and negative events. Some people may get stressed as a result of receiving a promotion at work and having new responsibilities. Others may experience stress when preparing for a dinner party when they have limited free time and their house is a mess. Stress levels can also be affected by external negative events, such as losing your job or health insurance, having a fight with your spouse, or gaining weight. Stress levels become unhealthy when your body and mind are constantly under pressure. Learn to be aware of your stress levels and how much you can handle without detracting from your performance.

Here are four effective strategies to help you spend more time stretching and less time stressing:

1. SCHEDULE YOUR PRIORITIES RATHER THAN PRIORITIZE YOUR SCHEDULE

Many people are tempted to make their schedule and then figure out what's important. The problem with this approach is the things that *are* important do not make it on the schedule. If you simply prioritize your schedule, there will be little time for the things that matter. If reading to your child is a top priority, you have to make the time. If working out is important, you need to schedule it in. Top 1%ers schedule their priorities so that important events make it on the calendar. Creating time for priorities is about being proactive.

2. DO IT, DUMP IT, OR DELEGATE IT

Your choices are either to do something yourself, dump it and forget about it, or delegate it. Too many people believe that delegating is impossible. The purpose of delegating is to free up time to focus on your priorities. It often involves giving up some control so that you can put your energy to better use elsewhere. You may be used to doing a task and think it is easier and quicker to do it yourself. This is the mindset that keeps you from delegating. Remember to focus on your strengths and empower others by utilizing theirs.

Initially, you may have to invest some time, but in the long run you will free up your mind. Keep in mind that when you delegate, it often helps someone else expand his or her role. Let's say your house is in disarray and you feel overwhelmed, but need to focus on other projects. Even if you do not have a housekeeper it may be helpful to hire someone for one day to come in and clean your house. This one step will free up hours of your time and reduce your stress.

3. SAY NO

Yes, that is correct. You do not have to say yes to everything that comes your way. You can only do something about your stress level if you pinpoint what causes your stress. Think about how stressed you are on a scale of 1 to 10 (10 being the highest). When you reach a 7 or higher, your self-defense mechanisms need to kick in. This means saying *no* when you are asked to take on too much or do one more favor. It is okay to take care of YOU INC. first. There is no better way to thrive. Sometimes the best choice you can make is to use the word *no* to protect yourself. When you start to prioritize yourself and make changes, some friends will support your new behavior and others will challenge you, so be prepared.

4. FOCUS ON THE PRESENT MOMENT

Children are rarely stressed because they live in the present moment. They do not worry if the playground will be closed or if they will have time to take a bath before dinner. They are present with what they are doing in the moment which keeps their minds focused.

When you are fully engaged in the present moment and focus on one task at a time, your mind is clear. You increase your stress levels when you obsess about something from the past or spend time worrying about the future. You can't change the past and you do not control the future. Identify the most important priorities and then tackle one at a time. Strive to stay in the present moment, and your anxiety and stress levels will be more manageable.

> **TOP 1% TIP:** *Exercise your option to say "no" to honor your priorities and reduce your stress. If you are invited to dinner but really need the time to relax and get organized, politely decline the invitation. Figure out what is most important to you before you respond to an invitation. Remember, by exercising your right to say "no," you are actually saying "yes" to yourself.*

BOTTOM LINE SUMMARY

RITUAL SIX: LIVE IN YOUR STRETCH ZONE
Move outside your comfort zone

There are three zones of action: the comfort zone, the stretch zone, and the stress zone. Top 1%ers choose to continuously move outside their comfort zone and avoid tipping over into the stress zone. They are effective at delegating, knowing when to say no, and managing any imbalances. They spend the majority of their time in the stretch zone. Top 1%ers are able to manage their stress levels and consistently perform at their best.

KEY PRACTICES TO HELP YOU EMBRACE THIS RITUAL

1. Step outside your comfort zone to experience personal growth in any area of your life.

2. Make yourself a priority and remember that you have the option to say yes *or* no to make the best choices.

3. Be aware of which zone you are operating in and make the necessary adjustments to spend more time in your stretch zone.

TOP 1% PEP TALK
Now you can see the finish line. Believe in yourself and continue to take one small step at a time. Next, we are going to add in resilience to help with the final push to the summit in Part III of the book.

IDEAS

PART 3: IMPLEMENT

Go confidently in the direction of your dreams.
Live the life you've imagined.

HENRY DAVID THOREAU

DRINK A CUP OF RESILIENCE

Our greatest glory is not in never falling,
but in rising every time we fall.

CONFUCIUS

Many successful people have failed on their way to success. The only *real* mistake is not learning from your mistakes. Michael Jordan, one of the greatest basketball players of all time, was cut from his high school basketball team. Because he was resilient, he went on to provide some of the most spectacular moments in sports history. He says, "I've missed more than nine thousand shots in my career. I've lost almost three hundred games. Twenty-six times I've been trusted to take the game winning shot and missed. I've failed over and over and over again in my life. And that is why I succeed."

Other top 1%ers have failed on their journey as well. Steve Jobs, the founder of Apple, was fired from his own company before he regained the helm as CEO. Oprah Winfrey was fired as a television reporter and then became a co-host of a morning talk show. Katie Couric, the anchor for *CBS Evening News* and former co-host of the *Today Show*, was told by a senior executive of the network, that she would never be on national television. A newspaper editor fired Walt Disney because he "lacked imagination and had no good ideas." Disney later started the theme park Disneyland, which was initially rejected by the city of Anaheim, California, because city officials thought it would attract "undesirables." Such stories can be seen in every industry. In order to succeed, you must meet failure or challenges with resilience. Failure is simply an obstacle. It is the end of one road and the beginning of another.

When you open a box of chocolates you decide which delicious treat you are going to bite into. You may pick the round milk chocolate with a fancy design on top, in the hopes of finding caramel in the middle. However, when you take a bite, you find a cherry filling instead. Will this experience stop you from trying another chocolate in the future? Doubtful. You throw away the chocolate and dig in one more time. When you want something bad enough, you will find a way to get it. In life, like a box of assorted chocolates, you do not know what you are going to get. Resilient people stay focused, regardless of the chocolate they choose.

RESILIENCE IS NOT ALL OR NOTHING

RESILIENCE DEFINED: *Your ability to deal with, overcome, and bounce back from unexpected obstacles on your path.*

Some challenges are in your control, like preparing for an exam or presentation, and others are outside of your control, such as your car breaking down. The true top 1%ers are resilient across the board—at work, in relationships, and in all endeavors. They leverage their best thinking from one area to the next, prepare for what they can, and think creatively to overcome obstacles.

You may be resilient in one area of your life, such as work, but need to be more resilient in your relationships. Luckily, resilience is not all or nothing. It is deeply related to mindset, specifically your belief system and how you interpret events. If you think a problem can be solved, you will work to find a solution. If you view something as impossible, you've just fueled that outcome. It takes practice to prepare for and overcome obstacles.

For more than thirty years, psychologists Emily Werner and Ruth Smith tracked 698 high-risk children who were born in 1955 in Kauai, Hawaii. The goal of their research was to understand why some children struggled while others, who were faced with a similar set of experiences flourished. The children grew up with poverty, abuse, lack of parenting, unstable homes, and alcoholism. Even with these circumstances, one in three children made it through and excelled.

What enabled the children to excel and overcome such hardships? They protected themselves by building strong relationships with other parental role models, siblings, and community support groups. They built confidence and subsequent resilience by experiencing small wins on their path. Resilience, like mindset, commitment, and setting goals, is a skill that takes effort and determination to perfect.

TAKEAWAY: Resilience can be learned.

RESILIENT OR NOT HERE I COME

Success is not final, failure is not fatal: it is the courage to continue that counts.

WINSTON CHURCHILL

The issue is not whether or not you think you are resilient; the issue is to increase your resilience as you move forward, regardless of your starting level. Recognize what you do well and identify what you would like to improve.

The following statements reflect resilient people. Read each statement and assess your reaction. The key is to be aware of how you think. If you lack skills in one area, then use it as a wake-up call to make some changes. Resilient people prefer to learn rather than find blame.

1. I receive feedback well.

2. I regulate my emotions in heated discussions or conversations.

3. I do not over emphasize the negatives in situations.

4. I see the positives in situations.

5. I keep things in perspective rather than magnify one event.

6. I believe in myself and am confident.

7. I learn from my mistakes.

8. I am optimistic and believe setbacks are temporary.

9. I bounce back from difficult situations.

10. I feel empowered when I hit a roadblock and design an alternate path.

Top 1%ers make the necessary adjustments in order to overcome challenges. They avoid taking things personally and refrain from dwelling on the negative in a situation. If a negative event occurs, they contain it as a local rather than a global event. If your presentation for an important client meeting did not go well, it means your presentation did not go well. It does not mean you are incompetent at your job or at giving presentations. Top 1%ers avoid internalizing external events.

People who search for the easy way out, by definition, are not resilient. The resilient ones are prepared and not easily swayed off course. Talent is helpful, strengths are important, and resilience is *essential* to bouncing back and developing YOU INC. into a thriving company. Opportunity awaits those who believe in themselves.

MY STORY (continued from the introduction): One day late in 2002, I got the call. I was working on Wall Street on the corporate bond sales desk. Everyone's face on the desk showed concern. My mind started to move a thousand miles a minute, but everything was in slow motion.

I stepped off the elevator on the eighth floor, and it was so quiet you could hear a pin drop. I walked into the office to find my two managers sitting quietly in a corner and a woman from Human Resources sitting at a table eagerly waiting to hand me my termination package. My managers did not say a word because of legal issues. They let human resources do the dirty work. I was not in control, and it was a surreal feeling. I was the most senior woman on the desk, and a logical choice to reduce head count and costs. I took my package, went back down to the trading floor, and asked a co-worker to bring me my coat, purse, and customer information. I did my best not to cry until I left the building.

I called my family and a few good friends and cried each time I shared the story. I was embarrassed, angry, and relieved all at the same time. I was used to defining myself as a Wall Street professional with friends, family, and new acquaintances. I could no longer hide behind my title. The title never reflected who I was, but it kept me from figuring out my true path.

Entering the world of unemployment was not easy. I was unsure of what to do next. I could have labeled myself a failure, but I tried not to magnify the incident. I called my clients and they offered their support. I took the rest of the week to collect my thoughts. I knew I needed to get back to my rituals and create a new schedule. My daily routine was drastically changed, and it took time to adjust. I started networking with friends, clients, and people from the industry. I maintained my fitness routine and started to enjoy going to the gym in the middle of the day.

My confidence was rattled and I needed some time to process the change and figure out my next steps. One of my clients encouraged me to interview at another top tier Wall Street firm where she knew the hiring manager. I gracefully declined. The job had become toxic for me and was not a creative environment for me to thrive. I disliked the early mornings, chaotic trading day, and necessity to be on the trading desk all day. I was not using my strengths and it was time to move on. I spent a few months in San Francisco to enjoy nature and an outdoor lifestyle. The short time I spent in California planted the seed that eventually gave me the strength to leave New York City and pursue my dreams. It was a small step that helped to cultivate my vision of a fulfilling life.

I returned to New York later that year and worked in two more corporate jobs before deciding I was ready to make a change. The process of living in your top 1% does not happen overnight. I knew these jobs were still not the ideal role for me because I wanted to have my own company. Rebounding from the layoff gave me the confidence that I needed to start my coaching business two years later. As I continued to notice how many people did not enjoy their work, I realized that the coaching field could be a viable business.

During this period of time, three things became clear to me: I realized I did not want a career in finance; I wanted a non-corporate lifestyle and job; and I wanted to live on the West Coast within the next five years. Largely thanks to my resilience, all three of these visions are now my reality.

TAKEAWAY: Resilience is about finding a way to continue moving forward even when it's hard to see the light. Believe in yourself and a clear path will eventually emerge.

FIVE STEPS TO BUILD RESILIENCE

Resilience is the key to success at work and satisfaction in life...It is the basic ingredient to happiness and success.

KAREN REIVICH and ANDREW SHATTE,
The Resilience Factor

Resilient people share similar qualities. They make a conscious effort to learn from past mistakes, overcome setbacks, and adapt quickly. You can use the following five steps to boost your resilience levels.

1. BRING AWARENESS TO YOUR THINKING STYLE

What do you say to yourself in a challenging situation? How accurate are your beliefs and conclusions? You need to know what you are thinking before you can expect different results. One set of thoughts leads to certain beliefs about what you can and can't do. This will never change unless you change the inputs—your thoughts. The necessity to live with a *can-do* mindset continues to be essential as you build your resilience levels. I have seen clients improve their resilience levels by bringing greater awareness to the lens they use to view the world.

2. SET MEANINGFUL GOALS

Think about the goals you set in Ritual Four, *Go For The Goal*, and why they are important to you. This is a challenging step and may sound counterintuitive, but goals give you something to look forward to. It is more likely you will persevere in the face of obstacles when the outcome is important and valuable to you. When you have something to look forward to and are optimistic, you believe things will work out. Remember to use small steps to measure and enjoy progress along the way.

3. LEARN FROM EXPERIENCES

Do you know someone who makes the same mistakes over and over? This is a self-fulfilling cycle. You must realize that you have a choice. You can either learn from your mistakes and adjust your goals accordingly, or stay on the same path. The best leaders, athletes, entrepreneurs, and companies use past experiences to shape future strategies.

You are not alone if you have a setback or make a mistake. The trick is to learn from a mistake or setback so you are better prepared the next time. Top 1%ers have off days, too, but they extract something from each experience that shows them what to improve.

> **TOP 1% TIP:** *Create a life lesson guide with your personal wisdom that you could pass on to your children or generations to come. Make a list of the top ten things you have learned from mistakes you have made and how they have helped you make a difference in your life.*

4. BUILD YOUR SELF-CONFIDENCE

Self-confidence helps you take that first step forward. You may be confident in some areas but not in others. Confidence, like resilience, is not all or nothing. As you experience wins in each area, you increase confidence levels. One client told me she was not self-confident in new social situations and therefore concluded she was not a confident person. I invited her to share situations where she was confident. Without hesitating, she shared examples of being confident with family, friends, and athletics. She realized her original conclusion was misleading since she was actually confident in many areas. As a result, she realized if she could develop confidence in some areas, she could in fact develop it in others.

5. STRENGTHEN YOUR RELATIONSHIPS

Relationships are your community and support system. Research shows that people working in adverse conditions are more resilient to stress and get sick less often when they have supportive environments and strong friendships. Invest the time to build and strengthen relationships with friends, community, family, and work. We all have problems or issues that are difficult to handle. Sometimes it's helpful to have a support team to share your feelings with and know that you will not be judged. There will be times when you need to vent and other times when a co-worker or friend can help you get back on track or offer some helpful advice.

Insanity is doing the same thing over and over again and expecting different results.

ALBERT EINSTEIN

BOTTOM LINE SUMMARY

RITUAL SEVEN: DRINK A CUP OF RESILIENCE
Rise up in the face of challenges

We are all faced with a series of great opportunities brilliantly disguised as impossible situations.

CHARLES SWINDOLL

Resilience is a process like anything else. It is not easy, but it can be learned. If you try once and make a mistake, incorporate the knowledge, and build new best practices. Each time you step over an obstacle, you gain one more data point that proves you can do it. You start to build your resilience resume and gain experience. CEOs gain expertise over time before they fill the top role. It is no different with your endeavors. Top 1%ers continue to seek out new opportunities. These opportunities often include challenges, and challenges require resilience. Higher resilience levels equal greater opportunities for success.

KEY PRACTICES TO HELP YOU EMBRACE THIS RITUAL

1. Redefine each failure as a learning opportunity.

2. Focus on where you *have* been resilient in your life. Each win will help you build confidence.

3. Start to notice and change the thoughts running through your mind. You can learn to be resilient with practice.

TOP 1% PEP TALK

Every person who has raised his or her hands in excitement and said, "I did it," has at one time been resilient. I know you've been resilient in some area of your life. Where can you be resilient now? Let's keep moving forward and make choices that help you build your roadmap to live in your top 1%.

IDEAS

PRACTICE THE THREE Cs:
CHOICE, COMMITMENT, AND CONSISTENCY

We are what we repeatedly do.
Excellence then is not an act but a habit.

ARISTOTLE

Why does one person go to sleep at 11 p.m. and another at 2 a.m.? *Choice.*

Why does one person follow through with his goal and another does not? *Commitment.*

Why do the best companies and athletes excel over time? *Consistency.*

As is true for completing any personal achievement, you need to choose your path, commit to your goals, and remain consistent with your thoughts and actions. You need the passion and desire to overcome obstacles and move closer to your goals, even on the toughest days. The most fulfilling part of the experience is often the journey itself, not the achievement alone. It is the sense of empowerment you gain from reaching for something outside your comfort zone and making it happen. You will need to practice all three of the components in the equation below to produce your best—two out of three will not be enough to reach your full potential.

Choice + Commitment + Consistency = OPTIMAL RESULTS

Most folks may never want to do an Ironman, but no matter what their dream is, there is no excuse not to go for it.
SCOTT RIGSBY,
the first double amputee to finish an Ironman

SCOTT'S STORY: The announcer in Kona, Hawaii, yelled over the screaming crowd, "SCOTT RIGSBY, YOU ARE AN IRONMAN." After sixteen hours and forty-three minutes, Scott had accomplished the unthinkable and become the first double-amputee in the world to finish an Ironman distance triathlon with prosthetic legs. He swam 2.4 miles, biked 112 miles, and ran 26.2 miles, finishing within the course cutoff time of seventeen hours. Amazing!

Scott was in a life-altering car accident when he was eighteen years old. His life would never be the same. He was riding in the back of a pickup truck when an eighteen-wheeler collided with his vehicle. He lost one leg in the accident and decided to amputate the remainder of his other leg after complications and twenty-six surgeries. Scott struggled through depression and financial issues before turning his life around and becoming an athlete. He made a choice to live in his top 1% and showed that people who overcome physical and mental challenges can achieve their dreams. Training for an Ironman is comparable to having a second job and requires doing a combination of extensive swimming, biking, and running workouts almost every day of the week. Scott has completed over thirteen triathlons and earned a spot on the 2006 USA Triathlon Team.

This extreme example illustrates that when you put your mind to something special, you can achieve personal greatness regardless of your starting point. An Ironman is a grueling physical and emotional race, but anyone can complete this race if you set a goal, take action, and stay consistent. Too often our initial response is, "Oh, I can't do that." The truth is, you can. It's not about age, money, time, or physical ability. It's about desire and the three Cs—choice, commitment, and consistency. Scott's achievement is an inspirational reminder that determination, the willingness to overcome obstacles, and the refusal to use excuses leads to fulfillment and success. Make a choice today to move forward with commitment and consistency toward a goal that inspires you.

CHOICE

If you limit your choices to what seems possible or reasonable you disconnect yourself from what you truly want, and all that is left is a compromise.

ROBERT FRITZ

Candy Lightner experienced a horrible tragedy when a drunk driver killed her daughter. Candy was at a major crossroads and had to decide how she would live the rest of her life. In 1980, she decided to make the world a better place and founded *Mothers Against Drunk Driving*. She inspired other mothers to join the cause and took on one of the most powerful industries in America. A group of volunteers with no funding and no political clout proved that you can make a positive impact if you so choose. Candy made a powerful choice thirty years ago. Partly as a result of Candy's actions, our society no longer tolerates drunk driving.

There are two parts to choice. The first is to realize that choices and results are related. They should not be viewed independently. Your choices are the inputs that lead to certain outputs. Therefore, you will need to align your choices with the goals you set earlier in the book. Do your choices support what you are striving to achieve? If you want to learn to cook, are you trying new recipes and practicing ways to sauté chicken or are you ordering take-out every night? If you want to get in shape, are you sleeping late and meeting friends for brunch on the weekend or making plans to go for a run? Life is a series of choices. Each set of choices will lead to very different results.

The second part is to identify what choices have the greatest impact. Where do you want to invest your time and energy? Do you want to spend thirty minutes deciding which salad dressing to buy, or three minutes on salad dressing and twenty-seven minutes deciding how to progress in your career? If you have a fifteen-minute conversation with a good friend, do you want to spend ten minutes gossiping about others or fifteen minutes discussing what's important in both of your respective lives? You have the choice to make a difference every day. Jim Collins in his book, *Good to Great*, artfully points out that "greatness, it turns out, is largely a matter of conscious choice."

You can choose your career, your friends, and how you take care of yourself. You can choose to wake-up immediately when your alarm rings, hit snooze, or not to use an alarm at all. The point is you make plenty of choices each day. Do not let your mindset warp your view of what is and is not a choice. Invest your time in choices that add the greatest value to YOU INC.

You can choose to ask yourself daily, "What can I do to improve my life?" You can choose to take action and practice certain rituals. You can choose to surround yourself with people who motivate, stimulate, and challenge you to think creatively.

TOP 1% TIP: Write one of your goals from Ritual Four on an index card and carry it around with you for one day. Every time you make a decision, look at your goal to see if your choices support the results you want. If your goal is to start a profitable business, do sleeping late and watching TV support your goals? This is a powerful exercise that will help you align your choices and actions.

COMMITMENT

There is a difference between interest and commitment. When you are interested in doing something, you do it only when it's convenient. When you are committed to something, you accept no excuses, only results.

KEN BLANCHARD

Your commitment levels are deeply connected to your choices, beliefs, goals, and values discussed earlier in the book. These levels vary depending on your priorities. You need to determine what you believe in, what you want to achieve, and how you want to live your life before you can decide if you're willing to commit. Fulfilling obligations are based on being proactive and taking the first step, sustaining your actions or motivation over time, and completing the process by taking the last step. Departing from this course will result in a less than ideal outcome.

Naturally, you have commitments in each area of the YOU INC. blueprint. Your daily schedule is filled with various responsibilities to yourself and others. You commit to arriving to work on time, helping a friend move, paying your bills, volunteering, taking care of your children, walking your dog, and even getting married. Some of these things you want to do, others you feel like you should do, and the rest may be things you think you have to do. Before these commitments were put on your schedule, you made the choice to add them. Remember, if you have too many unwanted commitments you give away your most important assets—time and energy. As a result, your true priorities and goals get relegated to second tier status.

At the end of the day, how do your choices impact YOU INC.? Is your calendar filled with unwanted appointments all day or do they add value to your life? Try this three-step approach to evaluate and fine-tune the commitments in your life:

1. KNOW WHAT'S ON YOUR PLATE

Make a list of all the commitments you currently have. They can be things you do daily (such as starting work by a certain time or picking up your kids from school), monthly (such as attending a group meeting for an organization you belong to or paying your bills), or yearly (such as getting a physical exam or attending a work or personal growth conference). Look at each area of the YOU INC. blueprint to make sure you include everything. You can use the *IDEAS* page to write down each commitment.

2. IDENTIFY THE VALUE OF EACH ITEM

Before you can make any choices, you will need to understand what value, if any, the items on your list bring to the table. We all have many commitments on our plate. Some of these enhance our lives and others drain our energy and require too much effort. Next to each commitment you just listed, add a positive sign if it adds value to your life and a negative sign if it detracts from YOU INC. Have you committed to start a book club or be the captain of your company softball team? Have you committed to lead a major project at work and organize a charity event? You may notice that some recurring monthly commitments such as paying for add-on services to your basic cable bill no longer make sense because you rarely have time to watch TV. Perhaps putting that money toward a gym membership or paying down your debt would align better with your goals. This is a great way to see the whole picture and create some next steps.

3. DECIDE WHAT NEEDS TO SHIFT

In a dream world, you would cross off the commitments from your list that you did not want, such as paying off a student loan or a mortgage. Although you may not be excited about paying your monthly mortgage, if buying a house is a goal then it only follows to have this responsibility. Notice if your commitments push you away from things that are important in your life or pull you toward them. Are you volunteering too much and not carving out enough time for yourself? You will need to examine the different areas of YOU INC. to see what needs to shift. For example, in the relationships area, you will notice that your friendships change over time. Are you spending time with people who are supportive and helpful or friends who drain your energy? This may be the perfect time to shift your energy away from some friends and spend more time with others who inspire you. As the CEO of YOU INC., you will have to be honest with yourself and make some tough choices.

Always take a moment to consider what is involved, how much effort something will take to complete, and if you want to invest your time in a specific commitment. Often we say yes because an invitation or idea to work on a new project sounds exciting at the time, but when you have to take action you are no longer motivated to stick with it. Frequently, your priorities shift and a previous commitment does not align with your goals. Other times, you realize that the project or action takes more time and effort than you thought it would to complete. Many things will sound like a good idea if you give them little to no thought. If you find yourself with an unwanted commitment, you still have choices. You can find another way to do it, dump it, or delegate it. Commitment is more than saying "yes" on day one. It is proven over time.

How important is commitment? It's important enough to Zappos, an online retailer of shoes and clothing, that the company actually pays new employees $2,000 if they quit within the first thirty days of employment. This strategy may sound counterproductive but Zappos thinks it is better to weed out uncommitted employees early rather than later. The company's culture and business strategy places a high value on commitment.

Moving into your top 1% will take commitment. Think back to a recent win in your life. Did you stay focused during the entire process or were you only committed on certain days when you felt like it? My guess is your effort level was pretty high. You will notice there are similarities in your ability to stay on course when you want to accomplish something that is important to you. These are the practices you want to reinforce in your life.

TOP 1% TIP: *Make a list of the ten commitments in your life that consume the most time. If you need help, look at your calendar to get started. Carefully review the list to make sure all your commitments are either conscious choices or ones that enhance your life. Making yourself a priority should be on your list.*

CONSISTENCY

If we want to direct our lives, we must take control of our consistent actions. It's not what we do once in a while that shapes our lives, but what we do consistently.

ANTHONY ROBBINS

Would you use the Google search feature if it worked only 65% of the time? Would you shop at your local grocery store if it were open only 50% of the posted store hours? You want consistency from others. How consistent are you?

Companies stay in business because they consistently produce results and good products. Starbucks, the world's largest coffeehouse, has consistently delivered a similar taste and experience in each of its locations. It opened its first store in Seattle in 1971. Forty years later, it has over fifteen thousand locations around the globe. The company has had some up and down years, but over time it has delivered a consistent product on which customers can depend. As a result, Starbucks revolutionized the coffee experience and how people spend time during the day.

Consistency is essential in every industry. U2 is one of the most popular music bands of all time because they have consistently delivered music that connects with people around the world. Four Seasons is a luxury hotel because it consistently delivers excellence. If it merely offered good service or provided just average rooms, people would neither equate the hotel with excellence nor would they pay more to stay there. News sources such as CNN are more frequently watched because they deliver reliable news and cover the top stories on a consistent basis. Disney has built one of the most recognized brands in the world because it consistently delivers entertainment value and a magical experience that is consistent at all of its theme parks.

The best athletes produce results over time because they are consistent in their training regimens and performance. Roger Federer, one of the best tennis players of all time, has won sixteen Grand Slam singles titles, the most of any male player. Federer worked hard to produce consistent results. He turned pro in 1998 and broke into the top one hundred in 1999, the top twenty in 2001, and the top ten in 2002. He reached No. 1 for the first time in 2004 and consistently held the No. 1 position for a record 237 consecutive weeks. It takes time and commitment to consistently deliver results. Consistency means showing up day after day and being consistent with your inputs and outputs. When you stop being consistent, your results will fluctuate.

The people who succeed in losing weight and keeping it off are consistent with their actions as well. New fad diets are introduced to the public every day. The reality is that modifications to your diet made for just fourteen days will only provide short-term benefits. In fact, 95% of all dieters will regain their lost weight within five years. One research group, the National Weight Control Registry, has studied over 5,000 people who have lost more than thirty pounds and managed to keep it off for at least one year. The results clearly show that people who keep their weight off share consistent practices which include: exercising regularly, modifying what they eat, making a lifelong commitment to healthy living, and keeping a daily food journal. If you alter these variables, you will change your results. The formula is simple. It's up to you to consistently implement it.

PRACTICING CONSISTENCY IN YOUR LIFE

We all know we should be consistent, but consistency is a trait that eludes many of us. Perhaps you set a goal to lose weight or to work out every morning. The test takes place the next morning when your alarm rings and the thought of working out does not seem as enticing as it did when you set your original goal. Although it's often a struggle to regularly do something in your life, the ability to be consistent is one of the core traits that separate the top 1%ers.

Consistency is not a fleeting emotion, but rather a trait that needs to stay with you both when you feel like doing something and when you lack the motivation. You need to focus on why taking a specific action is important and what value it will bring to your life. When you commit to something that is not a priority, it often follows that you will be inconsistent. This is the time to raise your game and make this year different than the previous ones. Use the following checkpoints and questions to help you make choices that will put your time and energy to the best use:

☑ Determine if the action supports a goal that is a priority in your life. Often people have trouble staying consistent because the goal they are striving to achieve is not meaningful or important. We highlighted these pitfalls in Ritual Four.

☑ Clearly define the action or thought you are choosing to do. It's hard to be consistent if you do not know what you are trying to achieve. Ask yourself if these actions are sustainable given all your responsibilities.

☑ Leverage the power of small steps. If you want to get up thirty minutes earlier each morning, start by setting your alarm clock ten minutes earlier for the first week. The next week, set it fifteen minutes earlier. If you move into new things slowly, you will have a better chance of sustaining your actions. If you find yourself feeling overwhelmed, you may be overextending yourself. If this happens, reassess your commitments and adjust them to focus your time on your top priorities.

☑ Be patient with yourself. Consistency does not happen overnight, but it will happen.

The goal is to reinforce the practices that enhance your life. Think ahead to determine what result you will get by repeating the same action over time. Some will be good and some may not be what you want. Remember to borrow from practices that strengthen YOU INC.

TOP 1% TIP: You can build your consistency levels by holding yourself accountable using a few simple steps. Send an email or call a good friend and tell them your goal and the actions you will do consistently for the next thirty days. Then, set a date to get together and celebrate your success. You will feel great when you match your words with actions.

BOTTOM LINE SUMMARY

RITUAL EIGHT: PRACTICE THE THREE Cs: CHOICE, COMMITMENT, AND CONSISTENCY
Match your words and actions to your goals

Taking action is an important step, but it may not guarantee success. Top 1%ers understand that the path to optimal performance requires a choice, commitment, and consistency. You will be faced with a series of choices at every step on your journey. Your commitment to your goals and the consistency of your actions will determine your results. To live in your top 1%, you will need to evaluate if your actions are effective. If not, it's time to fine-tune and ask three questions:

1. Do your choices support your values and goals?

2. Are you committed to changing your reality?

3. Are you being consistent with your actions and rituals?

KEY PRACTICES TO HELP YOU EMBRACE THIS RITUAL

1. Make choices every day that add value to your life.

2. Maintain a level of commitment that is as strong on the last day as it is on the first day.

3. Stay consistent with your actions to help you achieve great outcomes.

TOP 1% PEP TALK
You are so close. You've done the hard work and the summit is around the corner. You are ready for the final ritual.

IDEAS

RITUAL NINE

BRING BALANCE
INTO YOUR LIFE

The best and safest thing is to keep a balance in your life,
acknowledge the great powers around us and in us. If you can
do that, and live that way, you are really a wise man.

EURIPIDES

Balance is one of the hardest areas to master because there is no simple formula. How do you work hard, spend quality time with your family, contribute to your community, and make time for yourself when there are only twenty-four hours in a day? To make matters more difficult, just when you find the perfect balance in your life, something happens that can push you off-course: you're handed a new assignment at work, you have a fight with your spouse, your dog needs surgery, or you have to move because your lease is up and your landlord is raising the rent. One event can throw off your balance and make you feel your entire life is out of whack.

The term balance refers to the state of feeling centered. To examine what balance means in your life, think about how many things you can juggle at one time while still operating at your highest level. What most people fail to realize is there is actually a range of balance in which you can operate most of the time and still be your best. You have to decide what range works for you. The only way to learn your range is through trial and error, as it will vary for each person. Once you achieve balance, you can make decisions with a clear mind.

Life balance is not an all or nothing game. It is something that requires constant adjustment, much like the physical act of balancing on one foot. Perhaps the reason why so many of us feel unbalanced is that we compare ourselves to people who *appear* to live perfectly balanced lives. The reality is that everyone's situation is unique and everyone operates best under different conditions. For example, some people wait for the last minute to meet a deadline because they work better under pressure; others need ample time to prepare and would feel undue stress with a looming deadline. The objective is to have a process that helps you maintain balance over a lifetime.

BALANCING YOU INC.

Since all the areas in YOU INC. are connected, you may notice how changes in one area can positively or negatively affect other areas in your blueprint. This tug-of-war can create an imbalance if it becomes too strong. For example, starting a new job can have negative implications on your health and personal relationships. If you are working late every night or attending after work functions, it's only natural that you will have less time to workout, sleep, and spend with others. If relationships are a key factor to feeling stable, spending insufficient time nurturing this area of your blueprint will leave you feeling disconnected.

On any given day you may be faced with a trigger event that alters your normal routine and prevents you from thinking clearly. Your definition of balance and what is sustainable will vary at different stages in your life, as will the range in which you operate. When one area drags down the other areas of YOU INC. you will find yourself temporarily out of balance.

Each area of YOU INC. represents a pillar to your success. Combined, they make up your foundation. If you think about a building structure, it is best supported when all the pillars are equally balanced. The structure is in danger of falling, however, if three or four of those supports fail. Similarly, if too many of the areas in your blueprint are wobbly then YOU INC. will be unstable. You need to step into the CEO role of YOU INC. in order to decide what is working and what has to change.

BALANCE SET POINT

In a study of identical and fraternal twins, psychologists have learned that a relationship exists between our genes and our satisfaction in life, referred to as a *happiness set point*. *Time* magazine noted these findings in a 2005 cover story on happiness and well-being. The theory suggests we are born with a happiness "set point" similar to a weight "set point." The most important finding is that a large part of our happiness level, at least 40%, is within our control. Sonja Lyubomirsky's research further substantiated this fact in her book, *The How of Happiness*. We can apply the same principle to the concept of balance in our life. This principle implies that each of us has a balance "set point" and can control a significant portion of *our* balance levels. This new perspective will help you view your life in a much more manageable way.

To help make sense of this theory, think about people in your life. Some people have a lot going on, yet they always have the time to meet you for lunch or call to see how you are doing. These individuals tend to make time for a variety of competing priorities. They maintain a high level of balance in their lives, whether through a natural "set point" or through a conscious effort to increase the portion of balance within their control. Others, whose situations allow them to have more free time always seem to be too busy to get together or even return your phone call. Those who fall into the latter group are often out of balance, regardless of their schedule. Your balance level will depend on the framework you develop to move beyond your "set point."

BALANCE FRAMEWORK

The *balance framework* is a helpful tool for developing the portion of balance within your control. It includes three essential factors: *seeing the bigger picture, identifying non-negotiables,* and *making conscious trade-offs.* Employing this framework will increase your clarity, help you make better decisions, and allow you to reach your potential. If you are a master at seeing the bigger picture but disregard your non-negotiables or trade-offs, you will continue to feel off-balance. When you neglect any one of these variables you will experience pressure on YOU INC. The diagram on the next page shows the three factors that, when in sync, will strengthen your foundation.

BALANCE FRAMEWORK

© ALISSA FINERMAN

1. SEEING THE BIGGER PICTURE

Seeing the bigger picture is about taking a thoughtful approach to your life and understanding how each action relates to a specific outcome. Some refer to this concept as a vision and others as a long-term view. Regardless, it allows you to look at a situation from a different perspective. Our natural tendency is to focus on the day-to-day minutia. While it's easy to get stuck in the details of your life, it is essential to take a step back and ask yourself, "What is truly important?" Seeing the bigger picture allows you to see where you are going. It is one of the key practices that take you into your top 1%.

MARY'S STORY: My client, Mary, wanted to lose ten pounds and feel energized when she started her day. She also wanted to spend quality time with her new boyfriend and to be promoted within the next twelve months. She worked in the communications field and her boss often made last minute changes to the meeting schedule which required her to work through lunch or work late. As a result, she struggled to maintain healthy eating habits and balance in her life. She was unable to see that the simple act of missing lunch caused an entire chain reaction which altered her balance level:

1) Unexpected meeting scheduled » 2) Missed lunch » 3) Made an unhealthy snack choice » 4) Felt bad about herself » 5) Ate too much at late dinner » 6) Slept poorly » 7) Too tired to exercise in the morning » 8) Derailed from attaining healthy living goal » 9) Frustrated at work » 10) Spent less quality time with her boyfriend » 11) Felt disconnected from her boyfriend.

Mary's seemingly insignificant act of consistently missing lunch detracted from the other areas of her life. When Mary shifted her mindset to evaluate her challenges from a different angle she understood how the pieces of the puzzle fit together. She made three changes to increase her balance level: brought a healthy lunch and snacks, talked to her manager to plan ahead whenever possible, and started training for a 5k race with her boyfriend. Within six months, Mary lost twelve pounds, finished her first 5k race, and was on track for her promotion.

TAKEAWAY: When you are struggling to maintain balance, you need to refocus your lens by putting the details into perspective.

2. IDENTIFYING YOUR NON-NEGOTIABLES

Non-negotiables are beliefs, commitments, and values that you are not willing to compromise. Identifying and using your non-negotiables will help you clarify your priorities and make better decisions. Often, you compromise the things that are important to you because you are juggling so many priorities in your life. When you do not honor your non-negotiables, you begin to lose your sense of balance and your foundation begins to break down. If this pattern continues, you will compromise a part of yourself and, as a result, give less than your best.

For example, one client viewed her top priority as taking care of her elderly parents. She felt guilty if she took time to exercise or prepare healthy foods for herself during the day. Consequently, over time my client gained weight, developed high blood pressure, and lost energy. As soon as we identified her pattern and made her health a non-negotiable, she began to make decisions about food and exercise that were consistent with her long-term picture of health. These decisions, in turn, allowed her to regain her energy, care for her parents, and restore balance in her life.

You can have non-negotiables in every area of your blueprint. For example, when you wake-up in the morning, you most likely have a list of things you do automatically, such as brush your teeth, take a shower, and have your morning coffee. If you oversleep one morning and are late for an appointment, you still do these things. We all have a separate set of non-negotiables. The more consistently you practice them, the more balanced you will feel.

A few of my non-negotiables include exercising regularly, getting at least seven hours of sleep, and being on time. Your non-negotiables may include spending holidays with family, getting a yearly physical exam, being prepared for meetings, picking up your children from school, or only working for a company that is environmentally friendly. What are *your* non-negotiables?

The chart below illustrates examples of non-negotiables in each area of YOU INC. You can use the *IDEAS* page to help you create your personal list.

CAREER

1. Do what you love.
2. Work from home.
3. Travel less than once a month for work.

RELATIONSHIPS

1. Surround yourself with people who support and respect you.
2. Date a non-smoker.
3. Save Sunday nights for family dinners.

HEALTHY LIVING

1. Sleep at least seven hours per night.
2. Eat breakfast every morning.
3. Exercise four times per week.

FINANCES

1. Pay off a portion of debt each month.
2. Invest in your 401K plan.
3. Pay your bills on time.

FUN & CREATIVITY

1. Travel to one new place every year.
2. Spend time with people who make you smile.
3. Take your dog to the park every morning.
4. See a movie once a month.

PERSONAL GROWTH

1. Live in an environment that inspires you.
2. Hike once a week to clear your mind.
3. Write for twenty minutes each day.
4. Repeat your daily mantra.

Because everyone's circumstances change over time, you need to periodically reassess your non-negotiables. Naturally, your priorities will be different when you are starting college than when you are starting a family. For a circumstance to cause you to budge on a non-negotiable, it needs to provide ample benefits to YOU INC. Remember, you are the one who determines your non-negotiables.

TOP 1% TIP: *Refer to your list of non-negotiables. Place a check mark next to each one that you successfully practice. List the things that are preventing you from honoring these non-negotiables and write down one small step you will take to put them into practice. This simple exercise will give you a clear picture of what adds to and detracts from your balance levels.*

---

3. MAKING CONSCIOUS TRADE-OFFS

The third factor in cultivating greater balance in your life is your ability to make *conscious* trade-offs. We are all faced with choices and dilemmas every day. Many of us have had the experience of being reactive, rather than making proactive decisions, and suddenly realizing our life is not as we want it to be. Before you make any decisions, you will need to confirm what is important to you by focusing on your beliefs, commitments, and values.

For instance, one client with two beautiful children and a rewarding job had not talked to his best friend in over a year because he was too busy. His lack of attention to his core value of maintaining friendships was leading him down a potentially unfulfilling path. It is important to keep the bigger picture for your life in mind when you are striving to live in your top 1%.

Remember, you are the one to consciously decide what trade-offs, if any, to make.

"Trade-offs" exist in every area of your life. You have to be clear on your priorities for the pieces of the puzzle to fit together. For example, one client made a temporary trade-off to give up playing golf on the weekends for three months so he could focus on remodeling his home, launching a new product at work, and spending time with his wife. Three months later, my client was playing golf again and living in his beautiful new home. The golf course was still open and his golf buddies were happy to have him back. Top 1%ers make *conscious* trade-offs that support their goals.

The balance framework depends on your ability to make trade-offs or choices that align with your *tier one* goals and values. Consider the following questions:

1. What are my most important priorities?

2. What trade-offs am I willing to make?

3. Are these trade-offs aligned with my goals and values?

KIM'S DILEMMA: My client, Kim, was invited to a weekend getaway to celebrate her best friend's birthday. She had not spent quality time with these friends for at least six months and desperately needed the time away both to reconnect and clear her mind. However, Kim was conflicted because she had a year-end presentation to give to her most important client the next Tuesday. Her original plan was to spend her weekend preparing for the presentation. Kim's career and relationships were important pillars in her life and contributed to her feeling grounded. However, more recently she had been investing a disproportionate amount of time in work because of year-end deadlines. She expected this trend to continue as her company was understaffed and her sales territory had been expanded.

Some people might think the obvious choice would be to prepare for the work presentation and make plans to see friends another weekend. Kim felt it was essential to celebrate her best friend's birthday. She made a conscious choice to work late both Sunday and Monday night to make the weekend possible. She also came back early on Sunday to prepare for her presentation. In the short-term, Kim sacrificed some sleep and exercise but she was able to reconnect with her friends and meet her work obligations without making a long–term health sacrifice. Had Kim opted to postpone seeing her friends yet again, she would have been further along the unbalanced path of neglecting her personal relationships. The chart below outlines Kim's trade-offs:

POTENTIAL TRADE-OFFS		
AREA	PROS (+)	CONS (-)
RELATIONSHIPS	Connect with good friends.	Neglect personal friendships.
CAREER	Time away from the office to gain a new perspective.	Less time to prepare for a meeting.
HEALTHY LIVING	Need the time away to laugh and relax.	Increase stress levels because of less time to prepare, sacrifice sleep and exercise.
FINANCES	Take a short vacation without having to fly somewhere.	Spend money that she may not have.
FUN & CREATIVITY	Need a short vacation with friends.	Cancel plans Monday night to prepare.
PERSONAL GROWTH	Break up routine.	Neglect personal friendships.

Each person has a different set of non-negotiables and trade-offs. Some situations may be easier to solve than others. If one too many goals, priorities, or unplanned events are thrown into the YOU INC. mix, you can lose your balance. When you understand the bigger picture and you have clearly defined your non-negotiables, making conscious trade-offs will help you achieve greater balance in your life.

BOTTOM LINE SUMMARY

RITUAL NINE: BRING BALANCE INTO YOUR LIFE
Make conscious decisions

Balance is a difficult state to achieve and maintain. Your focus should be on cultivating balance in your life and understanding what range of balance is sustainable to live in your top 1%. This range will change at different stages in your life. There is no need to compare yourself to others because everyone's situation is different.

The factors in the *balance framework* will help to redefine balance in your life and help you make better decisions. You must always be aware of your priorities so you can be the driver rather than the passenger. You need to consider the bigger picture, identify and practice your non-negotiables, and determine which trade-offs are necessary in order to live in your top 1%.

KEY PRACTICES TO HELP YOU EMBRACE THIS RITUAL

1. Recognize you have the choice to implement a framework that increases your balance.

2. Determine if specific details are helping or deterring you from seeing the bigger picture.

3. Identify your priorities first and then decide which non-negotiables and trade-offs are essential to stay balanced.

TOP 1% PEP TALK
Congratulations on completing the ninth ritual! You've done the work and you deserve success. This is the time to explore what is possible in your life!

IDEAS

_____

_____

_____

_____

_____

_____

_____

_____

_____

CONCLUSION
YOU ARE CLOSER THAN YOU THINK

Things which matter most must never be at the mercy of things which matter least.

GOETHE

Living in your top 1% is about exploring your highest potential in all areas of your life. The practice is about expanding your mindset, increasing your awareness of what you *can* do, and taking action. You will have the choice to go for either good *or* great. Both paths take time and effort. Why not choose great? Remember, your personal best is closer than you think. Often, it's just a small shift in your mindset that leads to a major behavioral change. My hope is that these nine rituals have given you a new system to better evaluate what's important to you and make the best decisions. Once your strengths, priorities, and goals are clear, progress becomes a natural step.

Think of the journey as if you are going on a road trip in your new car. Parts of the road will be smooth and parts will be bumpy. You are driving toward your destination and it is called *Living in Your Top 1%*. This journey is about creating a fulfilling life that you love by assessing where you are, designing meaningful goals and rituals, and moving into action.

You have to decide if you are going to live your life as a *professional* or an *amateur*. Which status will you choose? To be a professional involves passion, commitment, and action on a consistent basis. Amateurs commit and take action just on the days they feel like it. You will have to make choices for either level. It is not about the results you achieve relative to someone else, but rather exploring the heights of your own true potential.

Now is the time to start managing your life as a full-time business rather than as a hobby!

WORKSHEETS/RITUALS SUMMARY

It always seems impossible until it is done.

NELSON MANDELA

ACTION PLAN
LIVING IN YOUR TOP 1%

*The greatest danger for most of us is not that our aim is too
high and we miss it, but that it is too low and we hit it.*

MICHELANGELO

W elcome to the *Living in Your Top 1% Action Plan.* You've
read the nine rituals and now have some inspiring ideas and
goals to pursue. A great place to start is exactly where you are.
This *ACTION PLAN WORKSHEET* will support you on your
journey and be a great resource to use as a refresher during the
year. The plan brings together the key exercises from the book
so you have them in one convenient place. It is most helpful
to refer back to this worksheet every three months, or more
frequently if needed. You will find that the areas in the YOU
INC. blueprint shift with time and need to be continuously
evaluated. It is important to be mindful of these shifts and
incorporate new insights into your plan as often as needed. The
best companies adjust their strategies over time to keep pace

with new developments in their markets and you will need to do the same to keep up with the changes in your life.

Do yourself a favor, instead of saying that you are *going* to do something, I encourage you to do it *now*. The action plan is most effective to execute when you are committed to make these rituals a way of life. If you put in the time and follow through with these steps you will see results.

Here are three *must-do* guidelines for best results with your action plan:

1. Carve out at least thirty minutes of quiet time to focus on you.

2. Choose goals that are important to YOU INC. and ones *you* honestly want to achieve. If the goal you set is not important to you, obstacles will push you off course.

3. Write everything down. When you put your words on paper, you will feel empowered and start to visualize where you are going.

ACTION STEPS: If you have already done one of these steps earlier in the book now is a great time to transfer your ideas to the *WORKSHEET* so everything is in one place and you can refer back to it.

1. ASSESS YOU INC. BLUEPRINT: Identify the six core areas in the YOU INC. blueprint and then rate each area on a scale of 1 to 10 for where you are today (10 represents that you are completely satisfied with the area). If you rated an area of 6, write down what the gap from a 6 to a 10 represents to you. Remember, you always have the option to rename an area in your blueprint or to add a new area.

2. IDENTIFY YOUR TOP FIVE STRENGTHS: Strengths are your building blocks for success and confidence. Think about how you can use your strengths as you pursue your goals and work to overcome challenges. One of my favorite ways to assess *strengths* is to take the VIA Survey of Character Strengths at www.authentichappiness.com. This is a free online method that will take twenty minutes. Many of my clients have benefitted from this step.

3. WRITE DOWN YOUR GOALS: Identify and write down the most important goals in each area. These should be based on the YOU INC. blueprint and close any gaps you noticed above. There is no limit to how many goals you can have, so write down everything that comes into your mind. Think about the things that would add the most value to your life. What would you love to accomplish in the next six months? Would you love to change careers, get in the best shape of your life, or learn to play the piano? The only thing you need to do is to make sure it's important to you.

4. FOCUS ON TIER ONE GOALS: Identify your *tier one* goals from the list you created in step 3. You may have many goals but this action plan helps you focus on your *tier one* goals first. You can use this same process to pursue any of your goals. The key is to focus on goals that are important to you and will have the greatest impact on YOU INC. Some of your goals may address a basic survival need such as finding a job and others may be pure pleasure such as planning a much needed vacation. Remember to consider how each goal you pursue will impact your ability to maintain balance in your life.

5. IDENTIFY CHALLENGES/SOLUTIONS: List the challenges for each of your *tier one* goals and match each of these with as many possible solutions as you can design. Once you know what your challenges are, you can focus on solutions to overcome them.

6. TAKE SMALL STEPS: For each *tier one* goal selected, brainstorm and write down the essential small steps to help you get started on your journey. When you complete the first few steps on your list, write down the next group that needs to get done. You will start to build confidence as you make progress.

7. SET A TARGET DATE: Include specific target dates to complete each goal. You're always better off when you have a specific date to achieve. If you do not hit your target date, do not get discouraged. The focus should be on making a quick adjustment and figuring out a new time frame. Setting a date is a helpful way to hold yourself accountable.

ACTION PLAN WORKSHEET

ASSESS YOU INC. BLUEPRINT		
AREA	**RATING**	**GOALS**
RELATIONSHIPS		
CAREER		
HEALTHY LIVING		
FINANCES		
FUN & CREATIVITY		
PERSONAL GROWTH		

FOCUS ON TIER ONE GOALS	DATE TO COMPLETE
#1 Tier One Goal:	
#2 Tier One Goal:	
#3 Tier One Goal:	

IDENTIFY CHALLENGES	MATCH CHALLENGES WITH SOLUTIONS
#1	#1
#2	#2
#3	#2

TAKE SMALL STEPS ON TIER ONE GOALS	
#1 Goal, Small Step:	Small Step:
#2 Goal, Small Step:	Small Step:
#3 Goal, Small Step:	Small Step:

WORKSHEET: GOALS TO THRIVE

Take the first step in faith. You do not have to see the whole staircase, just take the first step.

MARTIN LUTHER KING, JR

Setting effective and meaningful goals can be the difference between a good and a great year. What would you love to achieve this year that would put a smile on your face? Now is the time to do it and live in your top 1%. Enjoy the process and remember to write everything down! You can repeat these steps for each of your goals in the YOU INC. blueprint.

GOAL: _____

Why is your goal important?

_____

_____

What's the priority of your goal on a scale of 1 to 10 (10 is the highest)? _____

Which of your core values are connected with this goal?

_____

_____

What small steps will you take to make progress?

_____

_____

_____

What challenges/obstacles will you overcome on your path and how will you move past them?

_____

_____

_____

What other resources do you need to be successful (support team, progress markers, accountability measures, etc.)?

_____

_____

_____

When will you complete your goal?

_____

_____

WORKSHEET: RITUALS FOR SUCCESS

Your thoughts become your words. Your words become your actions. Your actions become your habits. Your habits become your values. Your values become your destiny.

MAHATMA GANDHI

Rituals help you reinforce positive mental and physical practices to perform at your highest and best levels. They help you develop new maps in different areas of your life to enjoy the results you desire. Spend a few minutes and write down specific rituals that you can practice on a daily, weekly, yearly, or consistent basis. It will be helpful to set rituals that support your goals identified in your *GOALS WORKSHEET* and *ACTION PLAN*. They will form the foundation to live in your top 1%.

A powerful ritual could be to assess YOU INC. in the beginning of every year, make yourself a priority each day, apply one of your top three strengths daily, think with a *can-do* mindset, take one small step outside your comfort zone each week, celebrate wins, call your family on the way home from work, save a portion of each pay check, or wake-up ten minutes earlier to schedule your priorities.

KEY QUESTIONS (repeat these questions for each new ritual):

What rituals will you start to practice?

_____

_____

Why is the ritual important?

_____

_____

What's the positive impact the ritual has on your life?

_____

_____

When will you start practicing the ritual and how often?

_____

_____

RITUALS TO START PRACTICING:

1.

2.

3.

4.

5.

6.

RITUALS SUMMARY

RITUAL ONE: BE THE CEO OF YOU INC.
Assess You Inc. on a continuous basis

The journey starts with you. Steve Jobs, CEO of Apple, looks in the mirror every morning and asks himself, "If today were the last day of my life, would I want to do what I am about to do today? Whenever the answer has been no too many days in a row, I know I need to change something." Living in your top 1% starts by investing in your most important asset—YOU. It's the most important business you will run. You need to fuel yourself on a physical, emotional, and spiritual level to be your best before you can give to others.

What's the most meaningful small step you could take for YOU INC. today?

RITUAL TWO: EMBRACE A *CAN-DO* MINDSET
Add the words "I can" to each challenge

Your words create your story. Your story creates your beliefs. Your beliefs create your results. The more you condition your mind and create a positive environment, the more you will flourish. Top 1%ers use their best thinking in one area and apply that mindset to everything they do. If you naturally think like a winner at work, and overcome one obstacle after the next, then apply that thinking to being fit, having strong relationships, and taking care of yourself. There are two words you need to adopt: *I can.*

What are the words or phrases that help you create your best self?

RITUAL THREE: EXCEL WITH YOUR STRENGTHS
Identify and use your key strengths

You can choose to focus on your strengths or your weaknesses. Both paths are a choice and will take time and effort to master. Using your strengths will bring you lasting fulfillment and success, while focusing on your weaknesses will keep you wondering why you are not making more progress. Focus on what you do well and address the weaknesses that matter to help you create a path to your top 1%.

What are your top strengths?

RITUAL FOUR: GO FOR THE GOAL
Set goals annually and take one small step each day

Goals are your ticket to living in your top 1%. They inspire you, give you something to look forward to, and make life that much more rewarding. The most fulfilling goals add meaning to your life and energize you.

Fast-forward six months. What is the one goal you would be thrilled to achieve?

RITUAL FIVE: THINK WITHOUT OBSTACLES
Visualize the ideal outcome

The best companies see opportunities when others see obstacles. Apple and Google are companies that innovate because they think about what can be rather than why something can't be. They believe in possibilities, see solutions, and are highly committed to their goals. They know there are obstacles on the way, but their vision is so compelling that the obstacles become speed bumps. Let your goal be to think without limits about what you *can* create.

What obstacles can you look beyond today to create an ideal outcome in the future?

RITUAL SIX: LIVE IN YOUR STRETCH ZONE
Move outside your comfort zone

Comfort zones are predictable. You know what to expect. There are no surprises, but there are also no rewards. You will reach the summit and enjoy peak experiences only when you step *outside* your comfort zone. Each time you take a step forward you build confidence. Top 1%ers are encouraged by the opportunities that wait just beyond the comfort zone in their stretch zone.

What rituals are essential to help you move outside your comfort zone?

RITUAL SEVEN: DRINK A CUP OF RESILIENCE
Rise up in the face of challenges

Your thinking style is your greatest asset and liability. You become your thoughts, and your thoughts dictate how resilient you will be. Resilient people focus on solutions and do not magnify negative events. They achieve top 1% moments by taking one step at a time and persevere in adverse situations.

In what area of your life are you ready to be more resilient?

RITUAL EIGHT: PRACTICE THE THREE Cs: CHOICE, COMMITMENT, AND CONSISTENCY
Match your words and actions with your goals

"Let's get together this Saturday morning and go for a walk." It sounds like a great idea on Tuesday, but when Saturday morning rolls around, you are exhausted from the week and need to rest. You call your walking partner to cancel. Another week goes by, and the exciting idea you had two months ago to get in shape is moving further and further away. Motivation ebbs and flows on your way to achieving your goal. What began as a positive idea becomes a hardship if you are not fully committed. The fuel that makes top 1% moments possible is your ability to transfer consistency in your words into actions on good and bad days.

What would you achieve if choice, commitment, and consistency were already part of the YOU INC. blueprint?

RITUAL NINE: BRING BALANCE INTO YOUR LIFE
Make conscious decisions

Balance is perhaps the toughest area to master because it is always changing. You're balanced one day and the next day you have a new project or challenge that interrupts your game plan. The *balance framework* helps you look at the concept of balance from a new perspective. It involves three factors: seeing the bigger picture, identifying your non-negotiables, and making conscious trade-offs. These elements help you increase your balance level and live a more fulfilling life.

When you let yourself dream, what's the big picture that emerges for YOU INC.?

FAVORITE BOOKS

A Path with Heart by Jack Kornfeld

A Return to Love by Marianne Williamson

Authentic Happiness by Martin Seligman

Create Your Best Life by Caroline Adams Miller

Emotional Intelligence by Daniel Goleman

Flow: The Psychology of Optimal Experience by Mihaly Csikszentmihalyi

Living in the Light by Shakti Gawain

Manifest Your Destiny by Wayne Dyer

Mindset by Carol Dweck

Positivity by Barbara Fredrickson

Quiet Leadership by David Rock

Soul Mission, Life Vision by Alan Seale

Start Where You Are by Pema Chodron

StrengthsFinder 2.0 by Tom Rath

The Art of Happiness by Dalai Lama

The Four Agreements by Don Miguel Ruiz

The How of Happiness by Sonja Lyubomirsky

The Inner Game of Tennis by Tim Gallwey

The Power of Full Engagement by Jim Loehr

The Seven Habits of Highly Effective People by Stephen Covey

NOTES

LIVING IN YOUR TOP 1%

Loehr, Jim and Schwartz, Tony. *The Power of Full Engagement*. New York: Free Press, 2003.

Martin, K.A. and Hall, C. R. "Using Mental Imagery to Enhance Intrinsic Motivation," *Journal of Sport and Exercise Psychology*, 1995, 17(1), 54-69.

McNamara, Melissa. "Olympic Edge for Weekend Athletes," *CBS News* online, February 17, 2006.

NBC live coverage of the Winter Olympics, February 2010.

www.PaulaDeen.com

RITUAL TWO: EMBRACE A *CAN-DO* MINDSET

Dweck, Carol. *Mindset*. New York: Ballantine Books, 2006.

Ewalt, David M. with Rose, Lacey. "Bannister's 4-minute Mile Named Greatest Athletic Achievements," *Forbes*, November 8, 2005.

RITUAL THREE: EXCEL WITH YOUR STRENGTHS

Best Self Exercise: Center for Positive Organizational Scholarship at the University of Michigan's Ross School of Business. www.bus.umich.edu/positive/pos-teaching-and-learning/reflectedbestselfexercise.htm

Fredrickson, Barbara. "The broaden-and-build theory of positive emotions," *The Royal Society Online*, August 17, 2004.

Rath, Tom. *StrengthsFinder 2.0.* New York: Gallup Press, 2007.

Seligman, Martin E. P. *Authentic Happiness.* New York: Free Press, 2002.

VIA Survey of Character Strengths:
www.authentichappiness.com

RITUAL FOUR: GO FOR THE GOAL

Fredrickson, Barbara. *Positivity.* New York: Three Rivers Press, 2009.

Lyubomirsky, Sonja. *The How of Happiness.* New York: The Penguin Press, 2008.

Miller, Caroline Adams. *Creating Your Best Life.* New York: Sterling Publishing, 2009.

Seligman, Martin E. P. *Learned Optimism.* New York: Pocket Books, 1990.

Jordan Romero live interview on the Today Show, June 4, 2010.

www.cnn.com/SPECIALS/cnn.heroes

www.en.wikipedia.org/wiki/Arnold_Schwarzenegger

www.gov.ca.gov

www.history.nasa.gov/moondec.html

www.jfklibrary.org/Historical+Resources/
Archives/Reference+Desk/Speeches/JFK/
Urgent+National+Needs+Page+4.htm

www.millercenter.org/scripps/archive/speeches/detail/3368

www.nikebiz.com/company_overview/

RITUAL FIVE: THINK WITHOUT OBSTACLES

Carswell, Sue. "Interview with Olympic Swimmer Dara Torres," *Women's Health*, November 2007.

Crouse, Karen. "Torres is Getting Older, but Swimming Faster," *The New York Times*, November 18, 2007.

Hsieh, Tony. *Delivering Happiness.* New York: Business Plus, 2010.

Ted Turner: "Person of the Year." *Time*, January 6, 1992.

www.cycleforsurvival.com

www.en.wikipedia.org/wiki/Club_foot

www.KristiYamaguchi.com

www.pbs.org/wgbh/theymadeamerica/whomade/
turner_hi.html

RITUAL SIX: LIVE IN YOUR STRETCH ZONE

Covey, Stephen. *The 7 Habits of Highly Effective People.* New York: Simon & Schuster, 1989.

Lester, Michael. "Can determined adversaries turn into friend foes?" *California Lawyer*, October 2008.

CNN.com transcripts from *American Morning.* Rick Sanchez interview with Jessica Grant, December 23, 2005.

www.en.wikipedia.org/wiki/Kenneth_Cole_(designer)

RITUAL SEVEN: DRINK A CUP OF RESILIENCE

Reivich, Karen and Shatte, Andrew. *The Resilience Factor.* New York: Broadway Books, 2002.

www.cominguptaller.org/report/chapter1-2.htm

RITUAL EIGHT: PRACTICE THE THREE Cs: CHOICE, COMMITMENT, AND CONSISTENCY

Grodstein, F., Levine, R., Spencer, T., Colditz, G.A., Stampfer, M. J. "Three-year follow-up of participants in a commercial weight loss program: can you keep it off?" *Archives of Internal Medicine*, 1996, 156 (12), 1302.

Kagan, Daryn. *What's Possible.* Iowa: Meredith Books, 2008.

Tony Hsieh live presentation at the Milken Institute, September 23, 2009.

www.atpworldtour.com/Tennis/Players/Top-Players/Roger-Federer.aspx

www.en.wikipedia.org/wiki/Roger_Federer

www.madd.org/about-us/history

www.nwcr.ws/Research/default.htm

www.ScottRigsbyfoundation.org

www.starbucks.com/about-us

RITUAL NINE: BRING BALANCE INTO YOUR LIFE

Lyubomirsky, Sonja. *The How of Happiness.* New York: The Penguin Press, 2008.

Seligman, Martin E. P. *Authentic Happiness.* New York: Pocket Books, 1990.

Wallis, Claudia, "The New Science of Happiness," *Time*, January 9, 2005.

ACKNOWLEDGMENTS

Although my name goes on the cover, it is only there because of the input, guidance, and support of so many incredible people on this journey. My brother and best friend offered the first words of encouragement on my first draft, "I like it." His words gave me hope and confidence that this book could develop into something special. He read endless drafts and offered to review as many as I needed. He was a sounding board on every decision, and there were many on this project.

I am grateful for having parents that helped me believe I could be and do whatever I could dream. Thank you for your encouragement and willingness to stay with me to the finish line and beyond. It means a lot to know how much you care.

A heartfelt thanks to many talented and supportive friends who read portions of the book and offered valuable and honest feedback throughout the process. I would like to express extra appreciation to the following people who helped me take this book to the next level: Kayla Allen, Craig Cignarelli, Stephanie Culen, Mike Daly, Michele Dugan, Jewel Elizabeth, Mary Grieco, Victor Lobl, Lori and Mike Milken, Bill Montana, Carlos Moreno, Amberly Morgan, Amna Nasser, Connor Raus, Siobhan Roche, Shiggy, Jonathan Simons, Deborah Stewart, Diana Vogel, Carol Yingst, and Carolyn and Katie Finerman. A special thank you to Lisa Zollner for her hard work and editorial insights. Your input was often the difference between good and great. I am grateful for everyone's support and generosity.

Thank you to my close friends who have been so encouraging during this adventure. You inspire me every day to continue to reach for my top 1%. I am fortunate to have you all in my life and hope this book motivates many people to reach a little higher.

ABOUT THE AUTHOR

Alissa Finerman is an author, speaker, and motivational coach. She loves to help clients achieve their goals and experience top 1% moments. She is known for her clarity, energy, and ability to redefine your potential. She uses her experiences as a life coach, former professional tennis player, and Wall Street professional to inspire people to think bigger and get results. She works with individual clients and speaks to corporations about achieving goals and developing one's potential. She traded in a Wall Street career so she could give back and inspire others to do what they love and raise the bar in their life. She continues to challenge herself and has completed a half Ironman and was ranked No. 1 in the United States Tennis Association Women's 40 Doubles in 2008 and 2009.

Alissa holds an MBA from the Wharton School, University of Pennsylvania and a BA from the University of California at Berkeley. She received her coach training from New York University.

Alissa lives in Santa Monica, California.

To invite Alissa to speak or consult with your company, please contact alissa@finermanliving.com.

Website:	www.alissafinerman.com
Facebook:	www.facebook.com/alissafinermantop1
Twitter:	www.twitter.com/alissafinerman

Made in the USA
Charleston, SC
28 December 2013